MING . . . MEISSEN . . . SEVRES . . . WEDGWOOD

All these names conjure up the history, beauty, and romance of porcelain. From the ancient courts of fabulous Cathay and legendary Japan . . . from the private factories of great European monarchs . . . from the skilled hands of individual artisans who flourished over three centuries . . . it's all here.

This detailed history of the development and styles of porcelain ranges from ancient China to 20th century Europe and America. It is comprehensive, and lavishly illustrated with drawings and photographs, as well as hundreds of makers' marks. . . .

There is much fascinating information and many examples of style and subject matter for guidelines in identifying your own (or to be purchased) porcelain. This handy pocket size is ideal for dealer or collector, expert or novice, to take along to flea markets, antique shows, or anywhere you go to look or buy.

Titles Now in **THE COLLECTORS LIBRARY**

FURNITURE by Renate Dolz

HANDBOOK OF BRITISH POTTERY AND PORCELAIN MARKS by Geoffrey Godden

NETSUKE by F. Aichele and G. Nagel

PORCELAIN by Renate Dolz

Look for them in

Also by Renate Dolz
and available from Popular Library:

FURNITURE

PORCELAIN

by Renate Dolz

From China to Art Nouveau—
Origins and methods, forms and patterns
of the great manufacturers and masters.

Translated from the German
by Maurice Kasten and Charles Choset

POPULAR LIBRARY • NEW YORK

Published by Popular Library, CBS Publications,
CBS Consumer Publishing, a Division of CBS Inc., by
arrangement with Wilhelm Heyne Verlag

September, 1977

Copyright © 1969 by Wilhelm Heyne Verlag, Munich, Germany
English Translation Copyright © 1977 by
Popular Library Publishers

ISBN: 0-445-04097-1

Original German title:
Porzellan

CONTENTS

INTRODUCTION

What does porcelain have to do with a baby pig? The word "porcella" in vulgar Latin means piglet, and in common colloquial usage denotes a round, high-arched snail shell, the cowrie shell.

As a child, I owned a shell like that, wonderfully smooth and shiny, delicately spotted, and with a little opening on the underside, seemingly made by tiny teeth. I remember clearly that I was fascinated by this remarkable object while at the same time always a bit disappointed that it wasn't a real snail shell, but only one made of porcelain.

Over seven hundred years ago, probably even before Marco Polo's journey, a European merchant on his first visit to China, seeing for the first time China's precious glazed vessels, very likely thought of the name of the "porcella" shell. Perhaps he had become acquainted with cowrie shells as a medium of exchange. Marco Polo was the first actually to tell about "porcellana." After his return home in 1292, his account of his adventures in China threw his contemporaries into incredulous amazement. Along with his uncle and father, in 1271 he had undertaken a commercial journey (not unusual for the Venetians and the Genoese) to Peking (that *was* unusual), and for almost twenty years had remained as governor of a province in the service of Kublai Khan, a grandson of Genghis Khan and the Mongol who was the first Chinese emperor of the Yüan dynasty.

The flow of porcelain from China to Europe was sporadic at first. Attempts were made to imitate it by the Italians who were already familiar with the arts of faience and glass enameling, but the time wasn't ripe yet. Not until the sixteenth and seventeenth centuries did Europeans grow interested in porcelain, and then it developed into a passion.

On the other hand, porcelain trade between the Near East and the Far East flourished. A beautiful example is in the great porcelain collection of the sultan in the old seraglio (Topkapi) in Istanbul. Many pale green plates and bowls of the Sung and Yüan periods, as well as precious blue-and-white porcelains from the earlier Ming period, make up the most valuable part of the collection.

With the increase in the number of trips of exploration and the ever-greater number of companies founded by firms exploiting sea routes in order to establish branches in foreign lands (East India companies, for instance), by 1600 Europe had all sorts of luxurious items from foreign lands: spices, precious stones, new kinds of wood, rare materials, strangely patterned carpets, furniture, and—porcelain.

Tea, coffee, and cocoa triumphed as luxuries, and precious porcelain was the appropriate receptacle for these desirable hot drinks. The handleless little cups known as "koppchen" in Holland, for example, were imported in enormous quantities.

It became the fashion to display porcelain ware in the home. On the shelves of massive Baroque cupboards and on mantlepieces sets of five vases were displayed as interior decoration. Delft made masterful copies in faience of blue-and-white Chinese decorative motifs.

More than anyone else, the royal families were seized by a passion for collecting china and other Chinese products. Porcelain, often in striking forms, seemed especially appropriate for the palaces of the seventeenth century. Cabinets were created for the display of porcelain, and "Chinese pavilions" were built. Enthusiasm ran high for small lacquered pieces of furniture, lacquer-work on furniture and on wall panels, and, indeed, for all forms of chinoiserie.

August the Strong, ruler of Saxony and from 1697 the King of Poland, put even Louis XIV in the shade with his passion for collecting porcelain. In 1717 he traded six hundred dragoons with the soldier-king of Prussia for porcelain vases.

On March 20, 1709, after a long, futile attempt to make gold, Johann Friedrich Böttger in Dresden turned his attention to porcelain and was able to report to his king that finally a way to make porcelain had been discovered. In 1710 the first European factory for genuine porcelain was founded in Meissen and soon achieved world renown.

After that, many manufacturing companies came into being, at first under royal patronage, later under private auspices. Some were able to remain active only for a short time; many others continue today. Their products mirror the changes in style from Rococo through Empire, Biedermeier, and Art Nouveau to our own time.

Thanks to the fortunate link between technique and art we can today recast all the achievements of a Kändler or Bustelli into new forms. In addition, the entrepreneurs, technicians, and artists of our time are involved in discovering new possibilities of form and technique. Porcelain is also included in this large-scale general development—especially what in this book we call "classical" porcelain.

WHAT IS TRUE PORCELAIN?

Porcelain is ceramic and, like faience, earthenware, stoneware, and simple pottery, is made of clay and baked. It can be utilitarian in its uses, ceremonial, or technological; it can also be fashioned by a Bustelli, for instance, into a work of art.

The Chinese, highly skilled in arts and crafts, gradually evolved porcelain out of stoneware. Those porcelain pieces, delicate, white, translucent, ringing to the touch, yet strong, reached their peak of development with the Chinese and surpassed every other kind of ceramic ware.

In the seventeenth and eighteenth centuries faience was often referred to as porcelain, for there actually had been considerable success in giving it a deceptive surface similarity to the real thing, but with the swift, ever-widening spread of real porcelain, faience was dismissed as "ordinary" or "false" porcelain.

The chief ingredient in the composition of porcelain is kaolin, a fire-resistant decomposition product of feldspar. Feldspar is also called *petuntse* from the Chinese *pai tun tse*, meaning small white bricks, for it was in this form that the Chinese manufacturers delivered it.

The Chinese say: "Kaolin is the skeleton and feldspar the flesh of porcelain." In the case of European porcelain the glaze is formed of a similar mixture.

The proportions of the elements making up the material, the so-called *arcana*, are obviously the well-kept secret of each manufacturer.

The higher the kaolin content of the material, the hotter must be the temperature of the kiln, and to that extent also will the piece being fired be harder and stronger. The European porcelain newly discovered by Böttger was harder than the Chinese, but it is for that reason that Chinese porcelain had the advantage of a richer palette of colors, for some colors can't withstand the high firing temperatures.

Most important of all is the careful treatment of the basic material, which is prepared with water. China certainly does not have the best kaolin clay in the world, but the skillful handling conceals the slightest defect. The perfection of Chinese porcelain extends from the most extreme delicacy of an egg cup to monumental bowls requiring the fusing together of several pieces.

After spinning on the potter's wheel, or being shaped in a mold, the piece must be allowed to dry completely. European porcelain is then put through two firings. The first is a less intense preliminary baking at about 900° C. which dries out the piece and gives it the necessary strength for further treatment, while leaving it porous and absorbent. After dipping in thin-flowing liquid glaze, there is a second baking in another furnace at a temperature that reaches 1460° C. As a result, the glaze adheres to the piece, which loses some of its mass and becomes white and as hard as steel.

Porcelain that is baked twice without a glaze is called "biscuit."

Chinese porcelain was treated somewhat differently. It was glazed while drying in the air, then subjected to heat reaching 1350° C. The low kaolin content didn't allow a higher temperature. Since it was possible to dip into the glaze only the smallest unbaked pieces, usually the glaze was applied with a brush or, better yet, by blowing. For this purpose a bamboo tube, one end covered by gauze, was dipped into the glaze and what clung to the tube was blown onto the piece. Incised, finely cut, or added patterns were applied before the glazing, while the piece was still damp. In contrast to the practice in Europe, freehand carved work was rare; for that reason molds were often used that shaped the entire object.

The kilns of ancient China and of Europe in the eighteenth century were usually tunnel ovens in the form of horizontal half-cylinders. The kilns were heated with wood, which caused some difficulty—at the end subjected to the direct heat of the fire it was very hot, whereas at the other end of the kiln, near the outlet that was connected to the chimney, it was substantially cooler. The most even temperature was in the middle, and so it was reserved for the finest porcelain. To avoid impurities or the quick effect of the fire, the pieces were placed in already-fired clay containers (saggers or saggars).

Fire is unpredictable, and controlling it is very difficult. One opening, through which the fuel was inserted, made it possible to observe the blaze. The flow of air was regulated through small openings in the arched roof of the oven.

In Europe this problem of variable temperature was dealt with by inserting clay cones that indicated the correct temperature. Since the end of the nineteenth century, the cones developed by Seger, which indicate the degree of heat, have done extraordinary service. In China there were brick pieces made of a special clay for the same purpose.

The blaze usually lasted several days, then slowly cooled.

By the end of the eighteenth century a round oven was developed in Paris which, by means of several layered spaces arranged one over the other, made it possible to utilize the various temperatures. Thus, the preliminary firing was above and the subsequent one took place below. In addition, the protective containers were first baked in the upper space.

Later, brown coal took the place of wood as a heating agent. Today the tunnel kilns are heated with oil, gas, or electricity, which guarantee a stable temperature, so that scarcely anyone now knows anything about the difficulties and uncertainties encountered in ancient China at each firing.

PAINTING, COLORS, AND GLAZES

If porcelain were left unglazed and unpainted, it could still completely fulfill its functions, but how much lovelier it is with brilliance and color!

The Chinese masters of ceramics had a wonderful understanding of glazes and painting, and the inspired results achieved wide appreciation. This beautiful game between unpredictable fire and great artistic talent accomplished genuine marvels. The Chinese masters became the unsurpassed forbears of European porcelain art.

Thanks to the lower temperatures (to 1350° C.), they were able to use more colors. One of the famous glazes is celadon, its color produced by iron oxide, which had appeared often on stoneware during the evolution of porcelain. The name comes from a character in the novel *L'Astrée,* by Honoré d'Urfé, published in Paris in 1610. The hero, the shepherd Celadon, always wore a pale green robe, which became the fashion. The colors of celadon glazes waver between a tender gray-green, a pale olive, a tone of jade, and a blue-green.

The various reds of the equally famous oxblood glazes (French: *sang de boeuf*; Chinese: *lang yao*) came from copper oxide. They are almost never completely uniform in color, in most cases being buff or greenish at the lip. The oxidizing process creates the green, so that often the result is like an apple, a red object with flecks of green. "Peachbloom" also belongs in this group.

The strongest colored glazes with cobalt blue are *clair de lune* and the darker plover's-egg blue.

In China gold was fired once, but in Europe it was baked again and then burnished.

Cobalt with manganese produced a lustrous black glaze, mirror black. A brown glaze was the result of iron oxide. A yellow lead glaze is the so-called emperor yellow.

There were, of course, many deviations and fine shadings. The graceful watered glazes were given their beautiful iridescence by means of oxidation, that is, through a rich supply of air to the fire.

Craquelé (French: fissured, full of cracks) came into being because the glaze had a lower expansion coefficient than the material beneath it. The Chinese achieved it toward the end of the seventeenth century in a simple way. Either a glazed vessel, before firing, was left out in the sun for a longer time than usual, and then dipped in cold water; or a purer porcelain earth was used for glazing. In that way the chalk content of the usual glaze was displaced by feldspar. The finer the porcelain earth was, the finer would be the fissures of the glaze in the fire. Often red chalk or watercolors were rubbed into the fissures.

We can also classify as an art of glazing enamel color painting. The Chinese designations, *san tsai* for the so-called three-color painting, and *wu tsai* for five-color painting refer to this category. Enamel coloring is a kind of glaze liquid that gets its colors through metallic oxide. It requires less heat than does the other glazing. The terms "three colors" and "five colors" need not be interpreted too strictly, for there can also be a greater or lesser number of colors. The essential difference is that the three-color painting is applied to already fired ware (called "biscuit") and then baked, whereas the five-color painting is an over-the-glaze kind of painting. The painting is applied to ware that is already baked and glazed, and is then baked in at low temperature.

In three-color painting, the colors were kept separate by raised lines as in the cloisonné technique on metal, but could also be placed directly next to one another, or kept apart through engraved or incised lines, usually in brown manganese. There was also enamel "on the biscuit" in only one color.

During the Ming period, turquoise, green, aubergine or

eggplant, and yellow were the favored colors. For the later pieces of the Ch'ing period, especially during the reign of the Emperor K'ang Hsi, it became the practice to classify them under their dominant colors as "families." The French scholar Jacquemart took up this idea, and so we have a *famille noire* (black), a *famille verte* (green), and a *famille jaune* (yellow). In this connection it is worth observing that the five-color paintings were also organized into families, and it is in this group that we have the powerful *famille verte* with green, iron-red, black, aubergine or eggplant, and blue.

At the opposite pole, in a gentle way, is the *famille rose*, which in China was called "painting in strange colors," *yang t'sai*. It was the result of contact with Europe and the use of purple of Cassius. It was precipitated from chloride of gold to obtain all possible shadings.

The "green family" and the "rose family" have quite different color tones. Whereas the colors of the green family are clear, transparent, and bright, those of the rose family appear usually opaque and dull. The other designation, *juan t'sai*, (paintings in soft colors), was especially appropriate to this art of decoration, which flourished during the reigns of Emperor Yung Cheng and Ch'ien Lung. Europe was living amidst the Rococo style, which also preferred gentle colors. Five-color painting differed from the low relief of European painting over the glaze through a thick application of color, which gave an effect of high relief. The Chinese were able to make this adhere to their limestone glaze better than to feldspar glaze. Their wonderful luminescent achievement in color has never been surpassed.

In spite of the beauty of multicolored porcelain, the ware with a single color under the glaze holds a special place all over the world, as, for instance, cobalt blue on a white ground. Who doesn't know Meissen's famous *"Zwiebelmuster"*? In China as in the Near East and Europe, cobalt blue on white was the dominant color. The Chinese were also acquainted with a red produced from copper oxide. This ran into difficulties in the baking, and easily became black. These problems were solved only with the passing of time. In this connection, blue withstood the high temperatures in which European porcelain was fired.

Painting required a very fine brush technique and a good sense of style. In Europe, it was applied on ware dried in the air before being baked. Since the ware was absorbent, the colors fused with it at once. A false brush stroke couldn't be corrected.

In China a blue under the glaze was frequently very beautifully combined with enameled color painting.

The difference between Chinese and European porcelain painting is very great. In Europe there was real painting; the colors were mixed and shaded, often quite naturalistically. The Chinese, on the other hand, set colors next to one another and often separated them by means of dark outlining. They conceived of painting as entirely decorative, which is what gives to their work its clear coloring and its tranquil effect.

HOW ARE PORCELAIN FIGURES MADE?

In the beginning, the artist makes a model in clay embodying his idea or ideas. This model is multiplied by reproductions, the usual procedure with porcelain, in which a piece rarely remains unique, unlike sculpture carved from stone. Mr. X in one city can purchase the same Harlequin from Nymphenburg as Mrs. Y in another city, and both can enjoy this small masterpiece.

Molds are needed for reproduction. Although the Chinese worked with clay molds, Europeans preferred gypsum. These models, often alive with motion (think of rococo shepherds and shepherdesses), usually are made in sections. Each gypsum mold consists of two parts into which the prepared porcelain material is firmly pressed. The two parts are then pressed together. Since the mold draws water from the material, the dried piece can be cleanly pulled away from the mold. Now the "embossers" come into action, known in old European factories as the "white corps." Their job is to smooth out the obvious seams left by the molds and to put together with porcelain mortar the individual sections of the figures. Extra items modeled by hand, such as leaves and blossoms, are only now added.

After the baking the decorators take over the figures to dress them up, so to speak, since with brushes they apply the elegant colors and designs.

SOFT PASTE PORCELAIN
AND BONE PORCELAIN

Soft paste, or frit porcelain *(pâte tendre)*, was developed in France. The porcelain makers of Sèvres brought it to such perfection that it strongly influenced the style of other manufacturers. However, soft paste porcelain is actually not a ceramic product, but by virtue of the way it is made is more like glass. Most significantly, the material contains no kaolin; because of the addition of chalk it becomes opaque and white, and can appear to be porcelain.

The combining of the material and the glaze is especially complicated. Nevertheless, the lower kiln temperatures permit the use of the most delicate colors, which become luminous in combination with the glaze, which is applied later. This isn't possible with hard porcelain. The ware is unquestionably soft and vulnerable, and as a consequence the glaze benefits strongly from the lead content. Soft paste porcelain in France, Belgium, and Spain was always expensive, and a carefully protected luxury ware of upper class society.

Bone porcelain, also known as bone china, an English discovery somewhat similar to soft paste porcelain, does come closer in manufacture to real porcelain. It is made of clay with chalk content, a feldsparlike mineral, pliable clay, and phosphate of chalk (bone ash and phosphorus).

English porcelain has always had great competition from the justifiably famous English stoneware that is associated with the name Wedgwood.

CHINESE PORCELAIN

The Dynasties

Chinese history is marked by the dynastic succession of emperors. Consequently, artistic epochs are named after these dynasties. Many emperors have had a great influence upon the development of art. That is particularly true in the case of porcelain because, considered especially precious, it was produced in the emperors' own workshops.

The dynasties important for Chinese porcelain are:

Shang	16th–11th centuries B.C.
Chou	1122–221 B.C. (until 771 early or Western Chou, thereafter later or Eastern Chou)
Confucius	551–479 B.C.
Han	206 B.C.–220 A.D.
T'ang	618–907 A.D.
Sung	960–1279 (until 1126 Northern Sung, 1115–1279 Southern Sung)
Yüan (Mongolian)	1280–1367 (1260–1294, reign of Kublai Khan)
Ming	1368–1644
Ch'ing (Manchu)	1644–1912

The markings carried by Chinese porcelain since the Ming period indicate the name of the reign of a particular emperor, for each emperor took office under a particular sign—*nien-hao* in Chinese. The markings are either in brush strokes or in the older form of a seal mark in the right hand corner. Often these markings were falsely and misleadingly applied, as, for example, when in later times a valuable product of a past epoch was copied. Thus, porcelain items made in the late Ming period were often copies of works from the early Ming period.

In addition to the royal markings, which were only applied in the emperors' workshops, there were, of course, the marks of private makers, but few of them were important. The markings of the royal workshop during the Ming and Ch'ing periods follow:

MING DYNASTY
1368–1644

Hung Wu, 1368–1396;
first period of markings

Yung Lo,
1403–1424

Hsüan Tê, 1426–1435;
high point of the Ming period

Hung Chih,
1488–1505

德 大
年 明
製 正

Chêng Tê,
1506–1521

靖 大
年 明
製 嘉

Chia Ching,
1522–1566, Blue period

慶 大
年 明
製 隆

Lung Ch'ing,
1567–1572

曆 大
年 明
製 萬

Wan Li,
1573–1619

化 大
年 明
製 成

成
化
年
製

Ch'êng Hua,
1465–1487

啟 大
年 明
製 天

Tien Ch'i,
1621–1627

年 崇
製 楨

Ch'ung Chêng,
1628–1643

CH'ING DYNASTY
1644–1912

治年製　大清順

Shun Chih,
1644–1661

熙年製　大清康

K'ang Hsi, 1662–1722;
1628–1726 Director Tsang
Ying-hsüan, Blue period

正年製　大清雍

Yung Chêng,
1723–1735;
1726–1736 Director Nien Hsi-yao,
Blue period

隆年製　大清乾

Ch'ien Lung,
1736–1795;
1736–1753 Director T'ang Ying,
Blue period, then decline

年製　嘉慶

Chia Ch'ing,
1796–1820

光年製 大清道

Tao Kuang,
1821–1850

豐年製 大清咸

Hsien Fêng,
1851–1861;
revolt of the T'ai P'ings

治年製 大清同

T'ung Chih,
1862–1873

緒年製 大清光

Kuang Hsü,
1874–1907

The individual parts of the marking mean:

reign of	化 大	great (ta)
year (nien)	年 明	dynasty (example: Ming)
made (chi)	製 成	emperor's signature (example: Ch'êng Hua)

27

From the Beginning to the Ming Period

The potter's wheel is one of the oldest artifacts of human culture. It was known in Mesopotamia by the end of the fourth millennium before Christ. Whether it later found its way to China can't be known with certainty, although it is more likely that the Chinese discovered it for themselves during the second millennium before Christ.

Long acquainted with the use of fire, the Chinese as early as the Chou Dynasty (1122–221 B.C.) had a thick gray stoneware that had porcelainlike qualities. Certainly by the third century B.C., at the time of the Warring Kingdoms (482–221 B.C.), they achieved the first water-resistant colored glazes. These were the foundations in technique for the development of Chinese stoneware and porcelains. The Chinese didn't *discover* porcelain, as in the case of Johann Friedrich Böttger in eighteenth century Europe; rather, there was a gradual development out of stoneware. This explains why we don't have exact information on the origins of their porcelain.

The ethical teachings of Confucius (circa 550 to 480 B.C.) had the widest possible influence at this time and formed one of the bases of the high level of Chinese art, which reached extreme limits of formal beauty, as well as affecting all areas of taste, culture, and the life of the spirit. Confucius and his contemporary, Lao Tse, the creator of Taoism, stand at the end of a world ruled by magic, the Chou regime, and at the beginning of a new time.

In 211 B.C. China was ruled by the Ch'in rulers who, since the beginning of the Han Dynasty (206 B.C. to 220 A.D.), had expanded the nation into a mighty power somewhat like the Roman Empire in Europe. The accomplishments in ceramics of this period are reflected chiefly in preserved grave objects such as models of houses and figures of people and animals in simple, powerfully expressive forms. The Chinese were also masters of bronze.

In this period came the first protoporcelains, of which the most notable products were the Yüeh ware with green celadon glazes from Chekiang.

In the following period, the so-called Six Dynasties Period (in actuality there were about thirty dynasties), only the Wei Dynasty had any ceramics of significance.

The first great period for all the arts and sciences came during the T'ang Dynasty (618–906). Buddhism, brought to China by monks during the first century after Christ, had extended itself everywhere and had reached every level of the population. For the first time there were large sculptures; some reached monumental proportions. A new open-door policy expanded trade with all East Asian countries. The capital city, Ch'ang-an, was an international meeting place, and China was the model for the whole Far East.

Trade in ceramics began during this period. Large-scale vessels glazed with strong colors, the underside sometimes untouched; beautiful small statues, glazed and unglazed, which we recognize as grave offerings; graceful dancers and servants whose clothes tell us about the fashions; saddle horses and camels which carry the possessions of their masters; the still much-valued Yüeh-celadon wares with delicate carved decorations under the glaze, especially popular in the Near East; and the first white porcelain—these were typical of the T'ang period. Unfortunately, social and political events, above all the arming of the peasants, led to uprisings. The greatest of these occurred in southern Hopei in 875, and ended the T'ang Dynasty. The Five Dynasties followed, and then the first Sung emperor.

The period of the Sung Dynasty (960–1279) is considered the classical period of literature, art, and science.

The standards set during this period remained unchanged for a long time. The man of learning was the ideal, and art was encouraged by the court. The emperor Hui Tsung was a painter himself. In such an atmosphere, great achievements were possible. The ceramics of this period are the most beautiful ever made in China, and later, during the Ming and Ch'ing dynasties, these simple, perfect forms with their elegant, generally monochromatic glazes were much imitated.

Wonderful stoneware was produced, equal in quality to porcelain. Among them is the *ju-yao* from the old capital, Kaifêng (modern Kaifeng) in Honan, with a blue shading from

Bactrian camel,
grave offering for Chancellor Liu,

glazed ceramic from the T'ang Dynasty
(8th century A.D.)

lavender to pigeon-gray as well as duck-egg blue applied in a crackled glaze (*yao*—originally oven-baked; later burnt or fired); also the *chün yao* from Honan in lavender blue with irregular flecks of blue-red. Through the use of copper, the green *chün* came into being; the crackled ware is the white *chün*. The *kuan yao* developed out of the *chün* and resembles it, whereas most of the white *ting yao* is real porcelain, delicate with a thin colorless glaze over an incised or carved pattern of flowers, birds, or fish. This ware was baked with copper, which accounts for a protective ring of bronze on the upper rim, the lower portion being glazed. With the loss of northern China as far as the Huai River in 1142 to the Chin, Hang-chou (Hangchow) became the new capital, and the kilns of Ting-chou were transferred to Ching-tê Chên. *Lung-ch'uan* ware from Chekiang first appeared at this time. The pieces are hard, gray-white and plangent, with celadon glazes ranging from pale gray-green to blue-green over incised leaf motifs and wavy patterns. *Ying-ch'ing yao* means "shadow blue"—the gently colored glaze appears darker in the hollows of objects. There was also *ch'ing pai* (blue-white) supposedly related to the legendary *ch'ai* porcelain, which was "blue as the sky seen through a break in the clouds after rain, clear as a mirror, thin as paper, and ringing like a jade tuning stone." It was produced in Kiangsi near Ching-tê Chên, the later porcelain center, and it is pleasant to think that the first blue-white porcelain derives from *ying-ch'ing yao*.

From the south China province of Fukien came *chien yao*, small conical bowls with a dark brown glaze usually striped or veined with a dark silver-blue, and known as "rabbit fur." Underneath, a brown section was left unglazed. In Japan this ceramic ware is called *temmoku* and since the thirteenth century has played a large part in the tea ceremony, which reached the Far East with Buddhism and in Japan reached a special perfection.

In Honan a charming glaze with small silver spots, the "oil spot glaze," was made.

Tz'u Chou yao is different from all the others. The forms are monumental, and the black painting under the glaze is very interesting, expansive, and suggestive of watercolors. From this ware came techniques of engraving and enamel coating.

As a brief example of the porcelain of the Mongol invaders we can cite the *shu-fu* porcelain, related to the *ying-ch'ing yao,* (shadow blue) which was produced during the Yüan dynasty in Ching-tê Chên.

In 1280 Kublai Khan, a Mongol, the grandson of Genghis Khan, overthrew the last Sung emperor and founded the Yüan dynasty.

The Chinese workshops continued to work in the old manner, and it is often difficult to know if a piece belongs to the Sung or the Yuan period. The forms of objects didn't alter perceptibly, but a new style of decoration developed slowly, perhaps influenced by examples of Persian red and blue under-the-glaze painting, taken in Kazan.

The Chinese adapted the discoveries from the Near East, and with their great knowledge of materials created their own blue-and-white porcelain. This style was at its peak during the Ming period and flourished again during the Ch'ing period. The paints were applied under the glaze in varied, broad sections and represented plant motifs, animal figures, and fabulous creatures. Some motifs came from patterns on fabrics or from old pieces that were imitated.

In 1325 there was an uprising against the foreign rulers, the Mongolians, which succeeded in 1368. As a result the emperor's throne in Nanking was occupied by the instigator of the revolution, the monk Chu Yüan-chang. He gave the new dynasty the name of Ming, which means bright, clear. He himself is known under the kingdom-sign Hung Wu (contained war-power).

The first period marks on porcelain appeared, and in 1369 in Ching-tê Chên, the former Ch'ang-nan-chên (now called Fowliang), since 800 B.C. the pottery capital, the emperor's factory was established. The geographical choice of Ching-tê Chên, to the north of Kiangsi, was auspicious for a pottery center; the necessary raw material was abundant in that area, and the breakable ware could be carried by water to the Yangtse River and thereafter with safety to the large export harbors.

Even in the Mongol period blue-and-white porcelain and *shu-fu* porcelain had been made there. Under Hung Wu a white ware was also manufactured.

Porcelain had by now taken first place among ceramics. It was under the protection of the emperor, and the emperor's workshops had to please the court. Only porcelains for the court carried the period marks. What reached Europe came not from the Emperor's factory but from the private factories at Ching-tê-chên.

The Ming period is divisible into three periods, each of which has its own pronounced character.

The period under the emperors with the kingdom-signs Yung Lo (1402–1424), Hsüan Tê (1426–1435), and Chêng Hua (1465–1482) we can call the classical period. A transition period under Hung Chih (1488–1505) and Chêng Tê (1506–1521) led to a quite different sort of era under Chia Ching (1522–1566), Lung Ch'ing (1567–1572) and Wan Li (1573–1619).

The periods of the last Ming emperors, T'ien Ch'i (1621–1627) and Ch'ung Chêng (1628–1643), mark a decline; nevertheless, the transitional porcelain made between the Ming and Ch'ing periods from 1619 to 1683 was much sought after under the name "traditional wares." Under Hung Wu, who had fought against Mongolian domination, there was little "official" porcelain, although private manufacturers developed the blue-and-white and the red-and-white and produced a good deal of celadon.

The young, weak grandson and successor of Hung Wu was without significance for the history of porcelain. A *coup d'etat* removed him, and one of his uncles took over from 1402 until 1424 as regent under the insignia Yung Lo (eternal joy). Under Yung Lo the famous porcelain pagoda in Nanking was built. Captain Crainville Loch saw it in 1842. According to him, there were white, yellow, red, and green pieces of porcelainlike tiles attached to the tower by mortar; the corners and reliefs with grotesque monsters were nailed on.

Although the more typical examples of porcelain were white, enamel coloring was known, and much delicate porcelain had designs incised under the glaze or painted in slip; these looked like watermarks when light shone through. Elegance of form is a hallmark of the early Ming period; by comparison, later forms appeared robust.

Blue-and white porcelain was dependent upon the availability of cobalt. Since the local product wasn't worth much, it was lucky for the history of porcelain that the capture of the East Indian islands by the eunuch Cheng Ho resulted in tribute from the conquered in the form of Somali blue, or Mohammedan blue, from Sumatra, which continued to reach China throughout the Hsüan Tê period.

Underglaze blue was the noted specialty of the age. Ming blue-and-white porcelain, in great demand at the time, may be the most beautiful ever made.

The Topkapi seraglio in Istanbul has a number of these precious pieces, in addition to many celadon items from the Sung, Yüan, and Ming periods.

The underglaze red also reached perfection. Like the blue it was used for designs that ranged over the entire vessel. The wonderful stem-cups with individualized red fish are completely extraordinary. A refinement that never slipped into decadence is the mark of the Ming period. Imitators were in thrall to it until the eighteenth century.

Hsüan Tê followed his model Hui Tsung, the founder of the golden age of the Sungs, in being well versed in art and interested in porcelain. He had an able director for his factory, Chang Shan. For the first time enamel painting was used, sometimes combined with underglaze blue.

After Hsüan Tê two of his sons ruled. In 1465 his grandson ascended the throne using the royal insignia Chêng Hua. He was a weak ruler, but his concubine, Lady Wen, had a love for porcelain, and thus gained significance for the Chêng-hua period in the history of porcelain. Overglaze painting (five-color painting with enamel colors) had its first brilliant age. When combined with underglaze blue, the resulting play of color was especially brilliant. Blue at this time had grown paler because only local cobalt was available. Painting itself began to change. There are palace cups in which one can recognize the transition to a new style with flowing, freely drawn tendrils in underglaze blue. This transitional phase continued until the Chêng Tê period.

Chêng Hua porcelain was very much imitated until the eighteenth century. Since reign marks are often absent, there are difficulties in attribution. Mention must be made here of the porcelain egg cups (t'o-t'ai, bodyless) of the period. In addition, there were the small, charming "chicken cups," much sought-after little cups decorated with hens and flowers.

After the Chêng Hua period, enamel-colored porcelain appeared more frequently.

During the transition periods under Hung Chih (1488–1505) and Chêng Tê (1506–1521) several new shades of yellow appeared: the light "emperor yellow" and "charming yellow." These were often combined as a color ground, with painting in overglaze blue. Also exceptional was a blue ground with white recessed designs. In the Chêng Tê period a blue and white porcelain with Islamic inscriptions was made. There were also beautiful pieces in painted enamel.

New imports of cobalt in 1520 resulted in the appearance in the late Ming period (beginning with Chia Ching, 1522–1566) of a luminous deep blue. It was during this period, including the reign of Wan-li (1573–1619), that porcelain makers were strongly influenced by Europe. A tendency toward a broader, less "penciled" style of painting, and scenes with people and animals in landscapes became more common, as well as forms in perspective. Under emperor Wan Li, who is said to have been extravagant and despotic, the amount of porcelain at court reached 34,200 pieces in one year, but the decorations lost much charm, and drawing and choice of color became coarser.

The transition period between the Ming and Ch'ing dynasties under the emperors T'ien Chi (1621–1627) and Ch'un Chêng (1628–1643) has a special importance for collectors and scholars. Many surprising objects made during this unstable time came from private workshops rather than the imperial factory.

There were fewer monochromatic glazes in the Ming period: Celadon maintained its pride of place, then came cobalt blue, copper red, and emperor-yellow; less frequently there were green and turquoise, and a great deal of white.

Among a number of private manufacturers of lower-quality porcelain, the one at Tê-hua (or Tehwa) in Fukien province is notable for one of the loveliest creations of porcelain art, the *blanc de Chine*. Tê-hua was the most important production center for this undecorated monochrome porcelain (cream-colored to white, also yellowish to rose) with its characteristic thick, lustrous glaze.

In this soft material, modeled figures are generally considered to be the finest work. The goddess of mercy, Kuan Yin, was repeatedly represented. She originally had embodied the reincarnation of the Buddha, but she became more feminine and took on the features of the madonna with the coming of the Jesuits. Also popular as themes for *blanc de Chine* were the hundred-armed Buddha; Lao-tze, the founder of Taoism; Putai, the laughing god of happiness, and the happy child, Hoho. There was every imaginable beast and fabulous creature. There were also miniature scenes from novels, people playing games, dancers, and Europeans (these often caricatured).

The Ch'ing Period

The weakness of the Ming states, civil war, and the arming of the people, hurried the conquest of the country by the Manchu Tartars. Their leader Abahai in 1636 gave his dynasty the symbol Ta Ch'ing, which signifies "great clarity," usually shortened to Ch'ing.

After the first emperor of the Ch'ing dynasty, who ruled under the name Shun Chih from 1644 to 1661, three extraordinary personalities followed: his son K'ang Hsi (1662–1722), his son Yung Cheng (1723–1735), and his son Ch'ien Lung (1736–1795).

Closely associated with the emperors' names and styles of porcelain are the names of the directors of the emperors' workshops. They were responsible for the quality of work done there. In 1682 after the rebuilding of the previously plundered, and partially destroyed, porcelain capital of Ching-tê Chên, Tsang Ying-hsüan was in charge. He was followed by Nien Hsi-yao (1726–1736) and T'ang Ying (1736–1753). With the retirement of T'ang Ying, the great period of Chinese porcelain drew to an end. The decline of the dynasty also began toward the end of the eighteenth century. The succeeding emperors Chia Ch'ing (1796–1820), Tao Kuang (1821–1850), Hsien Fêng (1851–1861), T'ung Chih (1862–1874), Kuang Hsu (1875–1908), and Hsüan Tung (to 1912) lacked the strength to deal with the persistent civil unrest. During the T'ai P'ing rebellion in the regime of Hsien Fêng, Ching-tê Chên was razed. The partial rebuilding in 1864 under T'ung Chih failed to restore the old brilliance. Finally, problems with European countries interfering in Chinese politics made normal development impossible.

Of course, today China continues to produce porcelain, but no new style has emerged. Production is limited at best to good copies of famous porcelains of the past.

The porcelain of the last great period is notable for technical virtuosity. It was a delicate, thin-walled porcelain without technical limits in its decoration. The pleasure in mastering the medium and its possibilities compensated for the risk of excess in matters of taste. Sometimes the decoration was overpowerful or strange or unsuitable material was used. On the other hand, there were many masterpieces.

This period strongly influenced Europe, but we can also trace the influence of Europe on China. Many pieces from the private workshops of Ching-tê Chên were made expressly for export, sometimes in response to commissions.

The models for imitation were the stoneware pieces of the Sung period and the porcelain of the Sung and Ming periods. However, an indigenous style developed as well. The severe, elegant forms of the time of K'ang Hsi are unmistakable. Very congenial to the baroque sensibility of Europe were the huge vessels which became show pieces. The lustrous colors of many new glazes brought the porcelains of the time widespread recognition in Europe.

Most prized was the *lang yao* (oxblood or beef-blood glaze), possibly named for the governor of the province of Kiangsi, who himself had a factory. These glazes ranged in color from cherry red and blood red to chestnut and to the rose colors of the famous peachbloom, or to bean-kernel red. Ashes-of-roses glazes with green flecks and brownish red glazes with rose splotches belong to this group.

Toward the end of the seventeenth century new green glazes appeared (with names like high-snake green, leaf green, and apple green) that were delicately colored and crackled.

There were monumental vases in blue and white and in

cobalt blue; other shades were powder blue (plover-egg blue) with gold painting and the pale lavender blue *clair de lune,* a glaze much loved in France during the time of Yung Chêng; and a deep blue glaze named Mazarin blue. Cobalt with manganese gave a shining, black glaze, "mirror black."

The celadon glaze remained one of the most beautiful monochrome glazes. Many of the old prototypes had etched decoration.

Of the yellow lead glazes, emperor yellow was still popular; new variants were eelskin yellow and sprinkled yellow. A lovely brown glaze was named *café au lait.*

The turquoise glazes differed little from those of the Ming period.

Blue-and-white porcelain from both royal and private factories was of high quality. The craftsmen now knew how to purify the local cobalt to get a good dark blue color. The painting was clear, without blurred lines and without the black specks which were present earlier as a result of impurities, and which were later intentionally added to copies of older pieces. Blue-and-white porcelain with a blue ground and spare white motifs was in great demand. Among the best known are ginger jars that have a blue crackled ground (like cracked ice) and white plum-blossom branches.

Enamel painting derived from knowledge of the late Ming period and was brought to perfection. Previously, three-color painting directly on the fired ware (enamel on the biscuit) had used the colors turquoise, aubergine or eggplant, green, and yellow, but during the time of K'ang Hsi large, elegant baluster vases in enamel on the biscuit with a black, green, or yellow ground were characteristic products on which blooming plants reached upward between cliffs. Porcelains are still classified according to their color ground as *famille noire, famille verte,* or *famille jaune. Famille noire* is popular with counterfeiters since a subsequent application of black can cover everything.

Porcelain figures, gods, pairs of Buddhist lions, birds, riders, youths as candle holders, phoenixes, and other smaller objects were mostly decorated in enamel on the biscuit using lively, eye-catching colors.

Five-color painting, produced a famous *famille verte* with green as the dominant color and iron red, black, and an enamel blue.

The motifs for painted blue-and-white porcelain were the same as for colored porcelain. Painted scenes with figures in a landscape or indoors, the three Taoist gods of happiness, harmony, and long life, along with symbols with similar meanings—bats, vultures, and insects—were frequent motifs. Also birds, blooming plants in rocky landscapes, and playful Buddhist lions and dragons always reappeared.

Painting full-scale pictures produced too strong an effect. Royal porcelain was more modestly painted. Porcelain for export was especially artful in its use of decorative borders. A new development was the process of "reserve" in which the background, say, is in blue while the design is in white, but the white actually is the color of the body of the porcelain, unpainted.

In 1712 the Jesuit Pierre d'Entrecolles visited the porcelain city Ching-tê Chên which at that time is said to have had a million inhabitants and three thousand royal and private kilns at work. His detailed account of the city, of the porcelain manufacture and its organization, remain to us in two letters to Father Orry in Paris in 1712 and 1722. The following excerpt gives us a picture of the assembly-line mass production of that time:

"The painting is divided up among a number of workers. One man paints nothing but the first color lines around the lower edge; another sketches the outlines of flowers, and a third fills them in. One man paints only water and mountains, another only birds or other animals. Human figures are usually assigned to the least experienced."

We learn from another passage that one vessel can pass through seventy hands before it is finished.

Besides painting, there were other kinds of decoration. As far back as the early Ming period there had developed the "secret decoration" (*an-hua*): through the application of slip, a design was produced which could only be seen when held up to the light, as with a watermark. In the rice-grain technique, a light, transparent ware was produced that had a perforated design filled in with glaze. The Japanese call this "glowworm" porcelain.

By the end of the K'ang Hsi period there was a marked

trend toward softer colors. At this time red and rose colors in all shades became popular. The *famille rose,* the "painting in strange colors" or "painting in soft colors" (in which gold and purple from Europe were used), was a notable feature of porcelain during the time of Yung Chêng (1723–1735) and that of Ch'un-lung until 1795.

There was always the danger in *famille rose* decorations of cloying, but the superb quality of the pieces from this late period help us to overlook that aspect. Since this porcelain suited the rococo taste of Europe, an especially large amount was exported.

The finest porcelain of the *famille rose* is associated with the name Ku Yueh-hsuan ("old moon terrace") and was at its best between 1727 and 1753. It was very rare and only made for royal use. Delicate flower stems, with and without birds, adorned the graceful bowls, cups, and dishes. There were also some pieces with landscapes, but rarely with people. There was always a lyrical poem added, sometimes from the emperor's brush, for Ch'ien Lung, a connoissur and collector of Sung stoneware, was interested in poetry and calligraphy.

The methods of production were lost with the death of the superintendent of the royal factory. After 1750 decline set in. Excess in decoration and superficiality in the choice of motifs became almost the rule. In 1912 the last emperor had to abdicate, and China became a republic.

The Symbolic Language of Chinese Painting

The beautiful painting on Chinese porcelain, whether in one or several colors, is not just decoration; it nearly always carries symbolic significance. A great deal of information is necessary to interpret correctly the combinations of different elements and transformations. Only some of the most important symbols will be indicated here.

One of the most conspicuous emblems in Chinese art is the dragon, a fabulous beast whose origin is to be found in the old snake cult and who represents a combination of rain and fruitfulness. The dragon is the royal coat of arms. In later times it was always shown with five claws.

Chinese dragon

The phoenix combines the features of the pheasant and the peacock. As the Chinese name *feng huang* shows, it unites the masculine *(feng)* and feminine *(huang)* principles. It is immortal and prefigures good fortune, especially a prosperous reign for an emperor. Five colors in its feathers signify the five cardinal virtues: Virtue, Truth, Selflessness, Wisdom, and Trust.

The *chi'lin* is a unicorn-like fabulous beast with a dragon's

Hoo-bird (Japan);
Chinese: *feng huang*, phoenix
(Old Kutani)

head and stag's hooves. Like the *feng huang*, it is a good omen for future success. Lions and the dogs of *Fo* were also represented more often than any other figures. They guard house entrances in pairs.

Chi'lin

Among human figures those of Buddha and Lao-tse are the most meaningful for Europeans, less so those representing the youth of Buddha, the sixteen Arhats or Lohans, and the Eight Immortals. The taoist Shou Lao, the god-like Lao-tze, appears as an old man sitting on a stag. The *ju-i* scepter or peach stands for long life. Putai, the god of happiness, is a well-fed old man, always shown laughing.

The goddess of mercy, Kuan Yin, is always a sculptured figure, typically in *blanc de Chine*.

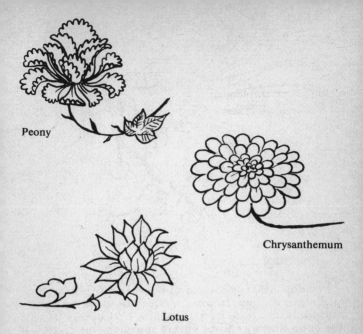

Peony

Chrysanthemum

Lotus

The animals and plants are all symbols. Several of them are usually grouped together, signifying good fortune and a long life: "Friends of winter"—pine, bamboo, and plum blossoms. Peach, lemons, and pomegranate indicate many sons. Seasons of the year and months are recognizable through flowers. Peony heralds spring; lotus, a symbol of purity, stands for summer; chrysanthemum, autumn; and the flowering branch of the plum tree, winter. Plum blossoms, symbols of unchanging beauty (since they appear before the leaves) are also signs of January; the peach tree (a Taoist symbol of paradise) of February. The peony is the sign for March, and the cherry blossom for April. May is represented by the magnolia, June by the pomegranate, July by the lotus, August by the pear blossom, and September by the mallow. Chrysanthemums, gardenias, and poppies are the symbols for the last three months of the year.

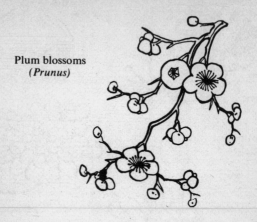

Plum blossoms
(*Prunus*)

In the animal kingdom, the rat means riches. The dog indicates something good to come; it is also associated with birthdays and marriages. Tigers and snakes hold sickness at bay. The horse is held to be the symbol of wisdom; the peacock is an expression of beauty, and butterflies and ducks in pairs mean good luck in love and marriage. Fish always bring luck. The bat appears frequently; the written symbol for its name when spoken is the same as good fortune (*fu*). In a play on words, stag (*lu*) can stand for a rich legacy; plum blossom (*me*) can be used for "again and again".

Bat

Yin-Yang, symbol of the
twofold creative principle

Shou, long life

Chang,
Endless knots—long life,
a Buddhist symbol

Numbers play a large role. There are the five virtues, five blessings, the eight jewels (Buddhist), eight precious things, eight geniuses, immortals, and musical instruments. Nine is the number for the greatest good fortune as in the case of the nine heavens.

Symbols are also used: The well-known Yin-Yang, a combination of the masculine Yang and feminine Yin, is symbolic of the twofold creative principle. It can represent the opposites of sun and earth (or moon), of fire and water, or heaven and earth.

The knot of *chang,* a Buddhist sign, like the sign *shou,* means long life. Good fortune *(fu)* also has its own special mark.

Doubling intensifies; not only similar symbols, but often different symbols with similar meanings are brought together. For instance, vulture and stag, which both mean advanced age, appear in the same design.

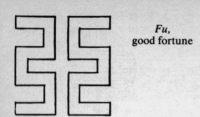

Fu,
good fortune

Lei-wên, thunder pattern

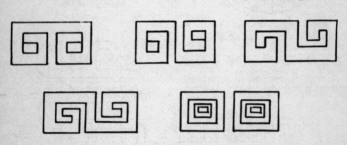

Among linear ornaments the thunder pattern *(lei-wên)* is the most common. It has a similarity to the Greek meander, which probably reached China through trade with India and Persia. The Chinese meander, unlike the Greek, was not continuous until the Han period. A spiral form was probably the oldest form of this ornament.

Clouds

Again and again we meet the clover-leaf design and wave and cloud ornamentation. Five-colored clouds indicate good luck.

Clover-leaf pattern

Waves

Large quantities of tendrils or swastikas were used as signs of limitless knowledge.

Export of Chinese Porcelain

The ceramic trade with other countries had begun by the time of the T'ang dynasty (618–907). In the fourteenth century under the Yüan dynasty the first blue-and-white painted porcelain was shipped out, and during the Ming period it was regularly exported. During this period the quality of the exported ware corresponded to that of the domestic porcelains. It was only during the Ch'ing period that a perceptible change in quality occurred. In any case, in the Yüan dynasty porcelain hadn't yet reached Europe. At that time the chief importers were in the Near East, and two famous collections exist that offer evidence of it. One is the porcelain collection of Shah Abbas the Great (1611) given to the shrine of Ardebil, which can be seen today in Teheran. The other is the already mentioned collection of the Sultan of Istanbul. Both collections possess early classic Ming porcelain in blue and white, and celadon from the Sung period.

Trade with Europe first developed in 1516 through the Portuguese and intensified when Portugal obtained a trade franchise in 1557 at Macao on the south Chinese coast. It was to the Portuguese market that the first porcelains intended for Europe were sent (Chêng Tê period, 1506–1521).

In 1600 the East Indian companies were established, and Holland grew interested in porcelain.

During the Ch'ing period trade spread ever wider, with England at the end of the seventeenth century taking the lead over all other European countries. The United States entered the scene in 1784. The porcelain for export was not always of good quality. Chinese private manufacturers began to accommodate the wishes of their patrons. The Dutch sent wooden models as prototypes. Every imaginable kind of mold or pattern was delivered to China to be imitated—beer tankards, apothecary vessels, fittings for holders of all kinds, silver and pewter vessels, and coats of arms for table service.

The Chinese filled all orders, copied pictures of buildings, hunting scenes, and classical and Christian motifs. Not only were there different European styles, ironically there were also figures from Meissen, with Chinese motifs and a Chinese point of view!

Mantelpiece garnitures and cupboard "crowns" in the form of five vases (three covered and two beaker vases), very popular in Europe, were manufactured, along with many small objects, in great quantities. Many were deliberately faked for export, as was Japanese Imari porcelain.

Traders in porcelain created resounding names for new types: "mandarin porcelain" (eighteenth century, decorated with costumed figures in over-glaze painting with purple, iron-red, underglaze blue and gold); "Batavia porcelain" (eighteenth century, painted in *famille rose* in panels on a ground of *café-au-lait* color); "Nanking" porcelain (eighteenth and nineteenth centuries, sea and landscape in underglaze blue), or "Canton porcelain" (eighteenth and nineteenth centuries, in underglaze blue, with ships and Chinese landscapes).

The peak of export trade was between 1760 and 1780, then the business cycle slowed. The market was surfeited, and European manufacturers became a serious source of competition.

The American market was active until the middle of the nineteenth century. For the Americans the Chinese provided (from 1780) a design, "Fitzhugh border," which united in underglaze blue on one piece the American eagle, *"mosaik,"* meander, flourishing branches, butterflies, and Chinese motifs.

Precious, rare individual pieces of Chinese porcelain were certainly brought to Europe quite early, but royal porcelain only reached Europe when the last Ch'ing emperor was forced to abdicate in 1912 and the palace was plundered. Since royal porcelain was intended only for the court, it was under no circumstances to be exported.

Many of these plundered treasures went to England, America, and Japan.

Typical Shapes of Chinese Porcelain

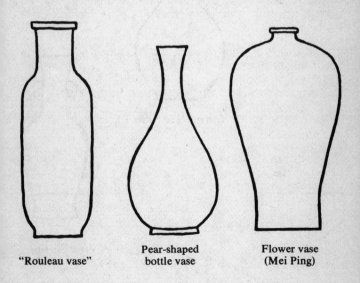

"Rouleau vase"

Pear-shaped
bottle vase

Flower vase
(Mei Ping)

Yen-Yen vase

Long-necked bottle

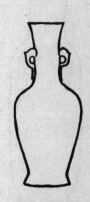

Vase with ring-shaped handles

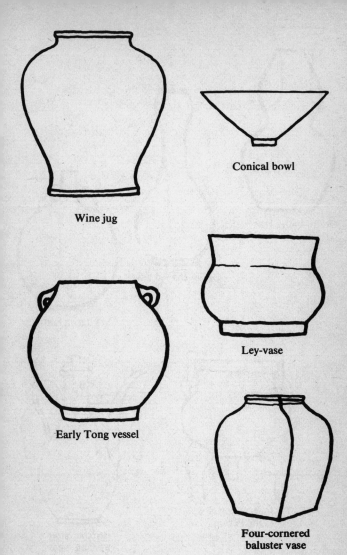

Wine jug

Conical bowl

Early Tong vessel

Ley-vase

Four-cornered
baluster vase

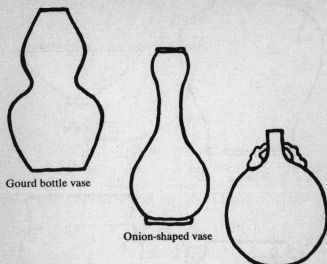

Gourd bottle vase

Onion-shaped vase

Pilgrim bottle

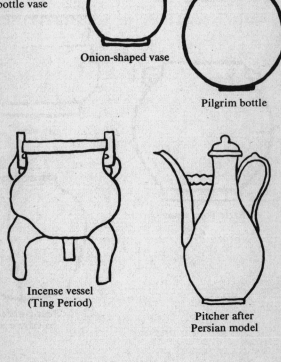

Incense vessel
(Ting Period)

Pitcher after
Persian model

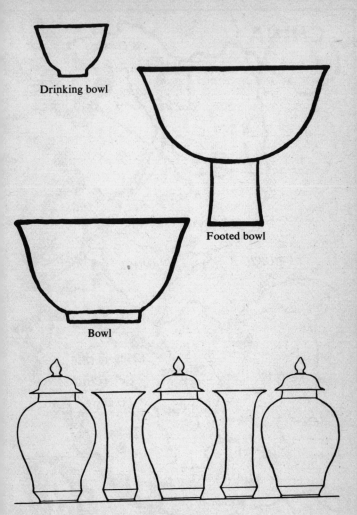

Drinking bowl

Footed bowl

Bowl

European favorite: mantelpiece garniture set
with two beaker vases and three covered vases

CHINA

Peking

Ting-chou ◎

HOPEI

SHANSI

SHANTUNG

Yellow River

Gr. Canal

Yello Sea

Chang-an

SHENSI

K'ai-feng

KIANGSU

Shêng-yang ◎

HONAN

HUPEI

ANHUI

Nanking

Yangtze River

Shanghai

Yüeh-chou

Ching-tê-chên ●

Chi-chou ◎

CHEKIANG

HUNAN

KIANGSI

FUKIEN

Tê-hua ◎

KUANTUNG

Swatow

Taiwan

Si-kiang

Canton

Macao

South China Sea

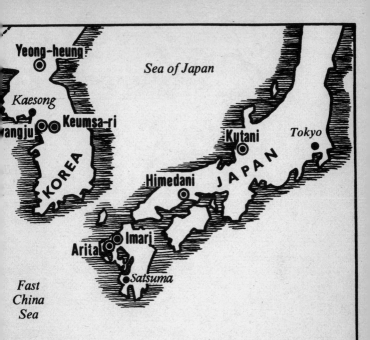

Yeong-heung

Sea of Japan

Kaesong

Keumsa-ri

angju

Kutani

Tokyo

KOREA

JAPAN

Himedani

Imari

Arita

Fast
China
Sea

Satsuma

Pacific Ocean

N

THE FAR EAST

◎ *Old centers of porcelain production*

KOREAN PORCELAIN

Korea was within easy reach of Chinese influence. As early as the Han period, 108 B.C., it was conquered by China. Nevertheless, a quite indigenous culture developed. Although affected by the impact of the Chinese, something characteristically Korean emerged. Stone work can be traced back to the sixth century after Christ, the Silla period, which lasted until 900. The following Koryo dynasty marked the flowering of Korean ceramics. In the tenth century a proto-porcelain was developed; in the eleventh century the first white porcelain.

Thirty-four kings ruled the peninsula in peace for nearly five hundred years (918–1392). This undisturbed sequence encouraged major achievements in nearly all areas.

The capital, Kaesong, was also the center of culture. Very fine celadon was produced there. Although influenced by the great Chinese classics of the Sung period, it had its own individuality. "Ice-bird glaze" refers to particularly beautiful shades of color.

Other characteristic Korean ware was baked in the one hundred fifty kilns of the eighteen ceramic centers: ceramics with inlaid designs under the celadon glaze; black or brown types painted under the glaze or covered with white clay (these based on the Chinese *T'zu Chou yao*); elegant tea ceramics like the Kómogai type with a fine, cracked ivory glaze; black glazed vessels named Korai Temmoru; and white porcelain of excellent quality. Typical of the decoration for all monochrome ware were stylized plants and birds, mostly made with hardwood molds.

The Yi dynasty (1392–1910), which replaced the Koryo dynasty, gave the country a long period of peace broken only by the onslaught of the Manchu Tartars and then the futile attempt from 1592 to 1598 by the Japanese general, Toyotomi Hideyoshi, to conquer Korea. Korean ceramics became known in Japan through the pieces carried home by the unsuccessful invaders.

As early as the fifteenth century, white porcelain in Korea had given way to the influence of blue-and-white and red-and-white Chinese porcelain painted under the glaze (Yüan and Ming periods). In Kwangju, southern Kaesong, these porcelain products reached notable heights and made for successful exports. But then Korean porcelain lost much of its own style under the broad impact of the Ch'ing dynasty, and with the end of the eighteenth century its decline set in.

China: Above, simple vessels of the classical Sung period, 960–1279

Above: From the Ming period (1368–1643): a small *blanc de Chine* vase with a carved lizard

Above: From the Ming period (1368–1643): the goddess of mercy (Kuan Yin) also in *blanc de Chine*

Above: Bowl from Tzu'chou (Hopei), Sung period, tenth century. Dark, watercolor-like painting on white clay, glazed

Above: Vase from the time of Emperor K'ang Hsi, 1662–1722

Above: Gourd-shaped pitcher with animal handles, Ming period, sixteenth century.

Above: Typical baluster vase of the K'ang Hsi period with climbing flower decoration in enamel painting, *famille noire*

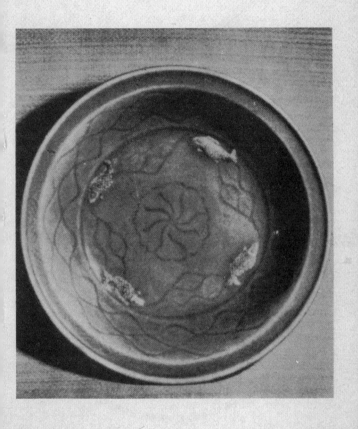

Above: Celadon plate, underglaze, etched decoration, applied
fish reliefs, Yüan period (1279–1368)

Above: Blue-and-white porcelain from the early Ming period, about 1420

Above: Blue-and-white porcelain from about 1650

Above: K'ang Hsi period (1662–1722), decoration in *famille
verte*

Covered vase, K'ang Hsi period, with *famille verte* decoration

JAPANESE PORCELAIN

Japan can also look back to a highly developed tradition of ceramics, which began with the arrival of Zen Buddhism and the first tea plants brought from China in 1200 by the priest Eisai. Zen, a form of Buddhist meditation developed in China, achieved in Japan its most individual, most profound form. Closely interwoven with it was the tea ceremony, the Tea Way, which led to enlightenment, and in which special ceramics were used. The Japanese potter Toshiro (Kato Shirozaemon Kagema) studied these tea ceremony ceramics in China and recreated them in Japan at the beginning of the thirteenth century.

The tea masters supervised the production of tea ceramics in specified colors and glazes and were responsible for the wonderful, simple forms which, developing out of the spirit of Zen Buddhism, matured into a special attitude toward the nature of ceramics. Tea ceramics were produced individually in small workshops.

Consequently, there was little interest in Chinese patterns, where ceramic manufacture was concerned.

The potter Gorodayu go Shonzui is said to have been in China during the Chêng Tê period (1506–1521) and to have brought raw material back with him, but production near Arita (Hizen Province) ended when the material ran out.

Only after the vain attempt by General Toyotomi Hideyoshi to conquer Korea did Japan manufacture porcelain. Hideyoshi brought Korean potters back with him. References can be found to Hideyoshi's "ceramic war". A Korean potter discovered suitable clay in Izumiyama near Arita, which (unlike the case in China) had the correct proportion of kaolin and petuntse (feldspar). In 1616 production began in Arita, and it continued to increase.

Meanwhile, in 1641 the Dutch, the only Europeans so permitted, established themselves on the island of Deshima in Hizen Province. With their help porcelain exports began to increase. Imari was the shipping port, and so the porcelain was called Imari. At first the blue-and-white porcelain made in Arita was under Korean influence. In contrast to Chinese porcelain, however, each item was subjected to a light firing before painting, and the Japanese potters propped up projecting parts by means of small clay cones, thus producing track marks.

The Japanese soon turned to enamel decoration, and the great potter and painter Sakaida Kakiemon (1595–1666) later worked only in this medium. He created the distinctive Kakiemon style, which, like the work of his followers who used the same name, was of the highest quality. The characteristic features were great economy in the designs, a great deal of white surface, "the formless form," and beautiful colors, sometimes in extraordinary combinations.

In 1646, for the sake of European customers, richer decorations were developed. This new Imari with its underglaze blue painting and overglaze iron-red and gold (previously rare in Arita) remained in good taste even though intended for export. It brought considerable acclaim, even in China, where it was imitated as "Chinese Imari." In the eighteenth century Delft, in Holland, brought out faience in blue, red, and gold, based on Far Eastern models. In addition, the Imari designs were copied in Europe on white imported porcelain.

Every educated Japanese was knowledgeable about Chinese pottery and Chinese writings, so Chinese motifs often were used on Japanese vessels.

Like the Chinese, the Japanese were fond of groups of symbols with fixed meanings. The bamboo was associated with the tiger, the peony with the lion, the acorn with the stag, and pines, bamboos, and plum blossoms together meant a fortunate life. Also dragons, peacocks, *hoo*-birds (phoenix), and quail were used frequently on Japanese porcelain. A popular motif for export was that of ships, modeled after Dutch sailing ships.

In Europe, Arita was the best-known and most important porcelain manufacturer. From about 1700 to the middle of the eighteenth century, Japanese porcelain was as much in demand as Chinese, and many enthusiasts collected it—for instance, August the Strong of Saxony and the Prince of Condé in France. The factories of both princes, Meissen and Chantilly, copied Japanese decorations with great skill and taste.

The other Japanese manufacturers were established by royalty and worked only on behalf of the royal houses. Their wares were not known in Europe until much later.

The factory of the House of Nabeshima was set up in 1680 in Okawachi, north of Arita. Along with blue-and-white porcelain with a very fine glaze, the factory made chiefly multicolored porcelains with underglaze colors of green, yellow, iron-red, and black, often combined with underglaze blue. Birds and plants were common motifs. Characteristic of the Nabeshima porcelain is a comblike pattern in underglaze blue on the rim of the foot of the dish.

A technically superb porcelain came from Mikawachi, south of Arita. The factory was established by the Prince of Hirado in the early eighteenth century. The work here was limited to underglaze blue painting, and used subtle Chinese themes. White porcelain decorated in relief with slip evoked memories of the Chinese *an-hua*.

Far from Arita, on the northwest coast of Hondo, lies Kutani ("new valleys"). The princely house of Maeda founded its factory here in 1640. Until the end of the seventeenth century a porcelain was produced here that had brilliant and beautiful enamel painting.

In 1824 there was a new development in Kutani. The opening of the ports to all nations in the middle of the nineteenth century encouraged exports, including imitations of old Kutani porcelain. Nevertheless, a new style of Kutani porcelain, with rich gold and red decoration, became famous as the "gold-brocade style."

Himedani in the prefecture of Hiroshima produced a good porcelain in the seventeenth century.

The decorative art of Japan twice influenced Europe, once in 1700 when lacquer-work and porcelain reached the Occident, and again in the middle of the nineteenth century when it gave impetus to the Art Nouveau movement.

PORCELAIN IN EUROPE

Johann Friedrich Böttger, His Predecessors and Followers

The enthusiasm of Europeans for Chinese porcelain, and its tremendous commercial implications, was a siren song drawing potters and alchemists in search of the secret of porcelain production. However, since nearly everyone worked on faience or its glaze as a point of departure rather than looking for the basic material (the right kind of earth), at best they only achieved the early stages of a pseudoporcelain, which is closer to glass than real porcelain made of clay with kaolin.

The Italians, especially, having long been makers of faience and glass, busied themselves with imitations. In the travel writing of Marco Polo (thirteenth century) there was a great deal about Chinese porcelain. In addition, Italians had done a certain amount of business with the Orient.

In 1470, the Venetian alchemist Antonio di San Simeone succeeded in making porcelainlike glass vessels. In 1518 a glassmaker in Venice, Leonardo Peringer, made a milky glass product with blue decoration.

The Renaissance, with the spreading of knowledge to all countries, sharpened the ambition of various princes to be the first under whose auspices porcelain was successfully produced. Francesco Maria de Medici, the grand duke of Tuscany in Florence, came closest. He himself pursued alchemical studies, and he succeeded with the help of Oratio Fontana and Bernardo Buonlatenti, a pupil of Michelangelo's, in making a porcelain-like, strong substance out of the white earth of Vicenza. This "Medici porcelain" had a bright yellow quality like stoneware, and like faience was covered with a white glaze containing zinc oxide. On this was baked a painting or design in blue or violet manganese, and then it was covered with a lead glaze and fired again. The potter Nicolo Sista carried on production of this ware in Pisa from 1576 until 1620.

In France, Louis XIV in 1664 first granted to the Parisian faience potter Claude Réverand, and then to Louis Poterat in 1673, the privilege of porcelain production, but neither Réverand nor Poterat succeeded in developing genuine porcelain. They couldn't reach the necessary high temperatures with their kilns. They are important, however, as the discoverers of artificial porcelain, which made the French manufacturers famous. The "soft paste" owes the splendor of its colors precisely to the low firing temperatures. However, because of its soft, porous lead glaze the ware was not appropriate for practical everyday use.

Pierre Chicaneau made a good artificial porcelain in St. Cloud near Paris, for which the king in 1677 granted him the royal privilege. After Chicaneau's death, in 1678, his widow carried on his work until 1766 with her second husband, Henri Charles Trou.

In the eighteenth century there were established the factories of Lille, (1771); Chantilly, (1725); Mennecy-Villeroy (1734); and Vincennes-Sèvres (1738). Sèvres became manufacturer for the State in 1753. Only in 1772, after the discovery of kaolin at Limoges, did Sèvres begin the production of hard porcelain.

In England Francis Place and John Dwight were on the right track, for they had started with stoneware, but Place lacked the money to carry his work forward, and Dwight had trouble with the Elers brothers, who had already produced a red stoneware (Elersware) and now contested Dwight's right to porcelain production.

Paris at this time was a crossroads for scientists, with the science of porcelain-making one of their preoccupations. The letters of the Jesuit priest Pierre d'Entrecolles of 1712 with his account of the Chinese porcelain center Ching-tê

Chên and its production methods excited great interest. The Dresden mathematician and physicist Ehrenfried Walther von Tschirnhausen met François Vilette of Lyon, the discoverer of the concave mirror, who had discovered means of achieving intensely high temperatures for melting glass. Vilette wouldn't give away his secret, but Tschirnhausen experimented with glass lenses, and succeeded in making something like porcelain. It was a soft porcelain that he named "wax porcelain." On May 25, 1704, August the Strong ordered him to work with the arcanist Böttger.

Johann Friedrich Böttger had been in danger in Dresden since 1701 because it was believed that he could make gold. He was born in 1682 at Schleiz, the son of a money changer. After the early death of his father, his upbringing was undertaken by Tiemann, the local administrator, engineer, and manager. At sixteen Böttger went to Berlin as apprentice to an apothecary. There he became infatuated with alchemy, which was at that time taken seriously as an important form of knowledge. Böttger hoped to discover the secret of making gold.

Friedrich I learned of the supposed success of the research, and since he needed money, he wanted to secure the gold maker for himself, but Böttger fled to Wittenberg in Saxony in order to pursue his researches in peace. He put himself under the protection of the Elector of Saxony, who first set him up in the fortress Königstein, then brought him to Albrechtsburg in Meissen.

In 1706 Böttger operated a laboratory in Dresden, along with fellow workers, dealing with this experimental research. Von Tschirnhausen belonged to this group. The new burning lenses stood the test of the heat experiment, but no gold appeared.

After 1707, on Tschirnhausen's advice, Böttger directed his attention to investigating the properties of earth. He was no expert, and perhaps because of that went about his business with no preconceptions or distractions. With the help of the high temperatures achieved with the burning lenses he brought different kinds of clay to the melting point. His first success in November, 1707, was red stoneware or "jaspis-porcelain" made of clay from Nürenberg and loam from Aue. It was brown and very hard. The model was the gleaming Chinese stoneware from Yi-hsien at Shanghai from which, as a rule, teapots were made. The color varied from pale yellow to dark brown, red-brown being the most desirable. It was being imitated at Delft in Holland and Staffordshire, in England.

The Böttger stoneware was produced for August the Strong, who expected something exceptional. The pieces were worked on by stone grinders as if they were precious stones; they were polished, buffed, cut, and faceted. They were gilded, or painted with lacquer colors, or given preformed ornaments—stylized acanthus leaves, or masks. The court goldsmith, Irminger, created molds. Some pieces had projecting sculpted figures from the *commedia del' arte,* or Chinese Kuan Yin, or plaques. It is thought that the great sculptor Balthasar Permoser, who worked in the Dresden tower, participated in this work with his staff.

A year later Böttger successfully created the first hard white porcelain and soon thereafter had a suitable glaze for it. At first the firing didn't always work, but Böttger steadily improved his material and kilns. In 1713 he found the brick clay that would hold the high temperatures.

The Meissen factory was founded on June 6, 1710. The precious "arcana," the secrets of porcelain production, had to be shared by Böttger with both directors of the factory, Dr. Nehmitz and Dr. Bartelmei.

On March 3, 1719, Johann Friedrich Böttger died in Dresden. He wasn't the only discoverer of porcelain in Europe, but he was the first. The discovery was in the air and, independently of him, success came to William Cookworthy in England, Dimitri Winogradow in Russia, George Heinrich Macheleid and Gotthelf Greiner in Thüringen, Lauraguais-Brancas in France, Vittorio Amadeo Giovanetti in Italy, and Frantz Heinrich Müller in Copenhagen.

THE MEISSEN MONOPOLY

For nearly half a century Meissen led in the development of the techniques and art of porcelain. They attempted strenuously to hide the precious arcana, the secrets of production. The men who were in on the secrets were sworn to absolute secrecy. Although employees were threatened with severe punishment if they tried to run away, or reveal the information, precautions proved futile. They tried repeatedly to give away or sell the secret. After all, what prince didn't have an intense interest in bringing porcelain to his country? As Duke Carl Eugen von Württemberg expressed it in his decree of April 5, 1758, on the founding of the factory at Ludwigsburg, porcelain "was a necessary sign of rank and dignity." And the private entrepreneurs hoped for profits.

In 1717 the Austrian councillor of war du Paquier, with the help of two craftsmen, the enamel and gold painter Christoph Hunger and the foreman Samuel Stölzel, both from Meissen, founded a factory in Vienna and began to produce porcelain. They were hardly offering competition to Meissen yet; however, Hunger soon left Vienna for Venice, where he founded a porcelain factory. In 1720 he returned to Meissen. By 1720 Stölzel also had gone back to Meissen, and had brought with him the gifted painter Gregor Höroldt. Because of business difficulties, the Viennese factory was taken over by the state.

In the middle of the century grim warning signals appeared. Meissen, which had been doing well in spite of the heavy burden of filling commissions for the nobility free of charge, was in financial difficulty. The peripatetic workers who knew the production secrets, usually from Meissen or Vienna, carried these secrets from manufacturer to manufacturer. Woe to the entrepreneur who fell into the hands of an impostor and for his money received only faience. The artists, too, rarely stayed in one place for long. Their work, sometimes with one manufacturer, sometimes with another, in time developed a certain similarity. Many new concerns were begun after 1717, but not until 1746, in Höchst am Main, did a manufacturer succeed in creating a productive and profitable factory. Its founder was the famous painter Adam Friedrich Löwenfinck, a former Meissen employee, who got financial backing from two Frankfurt merchants. In 1747, Neudeck ob der Au, later Nymphenburg, was founded, supported by the Elector Max III Joseph; in 1751 Frederick the Great gave the royal privilege to the merchant Wegely in Berlin; in 1753 there was Fürstenberg; in 1755 the Strassburger faience and porcelain craftsman Paul Hannong received from Elector Carl Theodor von der Pfalz the authority to found a porcelain factory in Frankenthal; and in 1758 Elector Carl Eugen von Württenberg took over Ludwigsburg from private ownership two years after it was established.

In addition to these the largest and most artistically significant manufacturers, many smaller royal and private companies were founded, but they didn't last beyond the eighteenth century. An exception is the Thüringer factory, which is still in operation. It was set up with commercial foresight in a solidly businesslike way, and remained for a long time entirely under the direction of the Greiner family.

The French manufacturers did not have Böttger's discovery. St. Cloud, Mennecy-Villeroy, Chantilly, and Vincennes (founded in 1740) produced artificial porcelain. The factory of Vincennes was replaced by Sèvres in 1756, and Louis XV took it over in 1759. It was only after the discovery of kaolin deposits at Limoges in 1768 that Sèvres began to produce hard porcelain. During this period there arose, especially in Paris, many new manufacturers of hard porcelain. In Germany this became a time of crisis, and many manufacturers had to close.

In Switzerland the Zurich factories were privately set up in

1763, and Nyon was founded in 1781.

Italy's most important manufacturers were founded by royalty. In 1735 the factory of Marchese Carlo Ginori in Doccia at Florence was founded with the help of the Viennese Karl Wendelin Anreiter from Zirnfeld. The factory Capodimonte was founded at Naples in 1743 by Karl III of Sicily, who had married a daughter of August III of Saxony and Poland. When Charles III ascended the Spanish throne, he moved his entire factory and staff to Buen Retiro at Madrid, and in 1804 hard porcelain was produced there, too. Ferdinand IV, King of Naples, established a factory in 1771.

England's factories produced mostly bone china, but later also took up hard porcelain. All the factories in England were started through private initiative. Chelsea, founded in 1743, merged with Derby in 1770; they were joined after 1776 by the manufacturer Bow. Bristol and Worcester were founded in the middle of the eighteenth century and after them many successful small factories. Etruria, founded by Josiah Wedgwood in 1768, later produced bone china as well as the famous Wedgwood stoneware.

In Belgium in 1771, Tournay, sponsored by Maria Theresa, was founded by F. J. Peterinck in imitation of Sèvres.

Holland's factories at Weesp, Oude-Loosdrecht (later in Ouder-Amstel) and Haag manufactured hard porcelain.

In Copenhagen hard porcelain appeared first in 1773, and then the factory came under state ownership.

In Russia there had been the manufacturer St. Petersburg, since 1744 helped by Christoph Conrad Hunger, and supported by Catherine II. Dimitri Winogradow independently discovered porcelain here in 1750. There were also several private entrepreneurs, such as A. G. Popow and the Englishman Francis Gardner, in Moscow. In all countries there were successful competing private companies even though the royally sponsored ones with their power and financial resources had the largest part of the market during this flowering of the art of porcelain.

The family Greiner in Germany had an especially lucky touch. Not only did Gotthelf Greiner manage to discover porcelain on his own, he and his five sons ruled the combined Thüringen porcelain industry during the eighteenth century.

In Zurich the family clan of Heidegger, to which the poet and painter of idyls Solomon Gessner belonged, founded a porcelain factory in 1763 that continued until 1790.

In Strassburg, Karl Hannong with his family had in 1710 been granted city permission to switch from tobacco-pipe maker to faience manufacturer. His products in Strassburg and Hagenau have a high reputation. His son Paul Anton wanted to make porcelain, but in France he wasn't permitted to compete against Sèvres. So he founded Frankenthal in Germany.

Two great entrepreneurs worked in England, William Duesbury, the porcelain king, and Josiah Wedgwood, whose previously mentioned stoneware had a widening influence upon porcelain. Both enterprises still function.

However, whether produced in royal or private factories, porcelain eventually had to be bought by, and brought to, the people. At all public events at which something was won or prizes given, and at the popular shooting matches, porcelain became the reward. There were porcelain lotteries and auctions. The competitive selling was sometimes carried so far that a country with its own manufacturer wouldn't allow the products of a foreigner into the country. Several Thüringer factories changed their markings to the Meissen crossed swords and brought their products to the Leipzig fair. Understandably, that didn't sit well, and not until mediation by the respective rulers could the wares once again be offered there.

Frederick the Great sent out a decree in 1769 granting Jews the right to marry, buy property, or open businesses only if they purchased a porcelain service from his manufacturer. This porcelain became popularly known as "Jew-porcelain." In 1787 the Prussian Jewish community was able to buy itself free of this forced duty for forty thousand talers.

In the Swiss cities, too, Jews were forced at betrothal to buy an expensive service from the Zurich manufacturer. Madame Pompadour called people who didn't buy Sèvres porcelain "unpatriotic."

At the request of the Turkish merchant Manasse Athanas, in 1732 Meissen made and shipped out many handleless cups with painted scenes of merchant ships. Meissen thus became the first European manufacturer to export to the Middle East.

This order of two thousand dozen of these "Turk-heads" was followed by more and larger commissions. In order to best competition from the Chinese, Meissen didn't hesitate to alter its markings—export porcelain carried stamp marks in imitation of Chinese and Japanese porcelain, instead of the sword mark of Meissen. Business flourished. Vienna in 1744 had many orders. Nymphenburg, in the years from 1769 to 1774, built a center for the painters of this export ware near Regensburg.

In spite of all this, the business activity of the manufacturers fluctuated widely. The pressure of competition was soon severe. By 1752 Wedgwood had made the first step toward mass production. His earthenware was decorated by a stamping process. His ware, while still good, was cheaper than that of other European makers.

Especially in Germany, burdened by petty difficulties among the many small states, there was a period of crisis, and a series of small manufacturers had to close down.

Ottweiler turned to manufacturing stoneware, and the great factories of Berlin and Meissen, like those of Sèvres and Petersburg, received subsidies in order to survive.

THE WARE OF
THE EIGHTEENTH CENTURY
AND ITS PAINTING

On January 23, 1710, the porcelain factory in Dresden was founded by royal decree; in June of the same year the permanent site of the Albrechtsburg in Meissen was fixed.

Böttger and his fellow workers constantly worked toward improving porcelain. The first Bttger porcelain designs hewed closely to Chinese models. They were also, on economic grounds, often in the same forms as earthenware, though attempts were made to move in indigenous directions, with the pitchers and vases being designed with reliefs of grape leaves or oak leaves, or acanthus, flowering branches, ornaments, and masks. Many pieces were white, but some were painted with lacquer, and a smaller number were painted with the still unperfected enamel colors of green, carmine, and blue. Böttger succeeded in creating a mother-of-pearl and a pink. He had less luck with underglaze blue, the color August the Strong wanted so much he offered a reward of a thousand talers for its discovery. A year after Böttger's death in 1720, the head master David Köhler and two co-workers did succeed in producing a blue color, but it was not entirely successful. In the same year the twenty-three-year-old painter, Gregor Höroldt, was engaged as chief painter in Meissen. He had been brought from Vienna by Samuel Stölzel, the repentant fellow worker of Böttger's who had returned to Meissen after he had betrayed the secret of porcelain production to Du Paquier of Vienna in 1718.

Two of Böttger's stoneware pitchers Meissen (1710–1715)

After a Chinese model

After a silver model

Höroldt, as painter, technician, and organizer, was a stroke of luck for Meissen. Under Böttger's lax leadership morale had weakened. Höroldt restored order and the financial stability of the firm. He worked to improve the colors that he had brought with him from Vienna, and soon had achieved almost every shade. His brilliant colors are typical of early Meissen.

But blue colors continued to be troublesome. Köhler had died in 1723 and hadn't explained his methods of producing it. In 1739 the problem was finally solved. In the same year there appeared the famous onion pattern *(Zwiebelmuster)* from a combination of pomegranate, asters, and Chinese peaches.

By 1731 forty painters were employed, with ten blue painters, twenty-five young apprentices, eleven children, and two color grinders who worked according to Höroldt's orders. Each had his assigned specialty: chinoiserie, landscapes, or flowers for which he was responsible—according to specifications, usually, though each could be individually creative. The young Adam Friedrich Löwenfinck, who later became so famous as a flower painter, at that time filled in the outlines of leaves.

Höroldt reigned supreme. He laid down the rules for the painters. In accordance with the wish of August the Strong that his Japanese palace (built by Pöppelmann) make use of Chinese and Meissner porcelains, Höroldt busied himself chiefly with Far Eastern motifs. However, his Indian flowers, which mixed lightly outlined chrysanthemums and peonies with fantastic birds in rare color combinations, were entirely his own creation and had little in common with Chinese models. They were replaced at Meissen in 1735 by the "German flowers."

In the creation of tea and coffee services, the court goldsmith Irminger had been an outstanding designer since 1710. He was aided by George Fritysche after 1712. In 1727 he delivered several designs to Johann Gottlieb Kirchner. The forms were mostly smooth, rarely with handles, and ornamented with small Baroque trimmings that looked like knobs. There was plenty of space for the painter's work.

The designs kept for the king, like the "Yellow Tiger" pattern and the "Red Dragon" pattern, reveal in their austerity Höroldt's awareness of Japanese Kakiemon design. However,

Zwiebelmuster in underglaze blue,
Meissen 1739

his name is more specifically associated with the chinoiserie of 1720. He hadn't discovered it, but he so amusingly and individually developed it that "Höroldt Chinese" became a descriptive concept. Running over the porcelain are animal-like, ludicrous figures in gold, or people with large hats and long thin beards. They are usually surrounded by strange dragons, flying snakes, or parrots in a fairy-tale world full of peculiar plants. Often these charming, unreal scenes appear in "reserves" (an area within a framing border) with gold-flecked designs on variously colored grounds. The wonderful ground colors—a yellow derived from emperor yellow, sea green, steel green, light and dark blue, peachbloom, gray, purple, and red— were the pride of Meissen. They originated in an idea of August the Strong of reserving a room in his Japanese-style palace for every color.

With the death of the king in 1733 the flowering of Höroldt

Indian flowers,
Meissen 1730

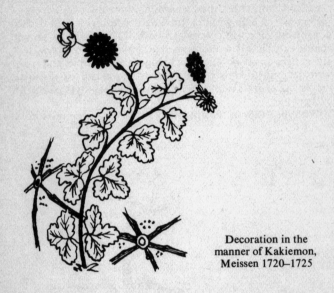

Decoration in the
manner of Kakiemon,
Meissen 1720–1725

painting was over. He created for the royal successors two
more famous services, the gold "Watteau" service and the green
"Watteau" service, but the great companion-initiator, under
whom Höroldt became the pathfinder for European porcelain,
was gone.

In 1731, twenty-five-year-old Johann Joachim Kändler
came to Meissen. With Kirchner, he was given the great task of
managing the Japanese palace. In contrast to Kirchner, who
couldn't adjust to porcelain, and who was temperamentally not
attuned to his royal patron, Kändler was made for this particular job. He could identify with the plans of the king, and
although he had been accustomed to working with large
sculptures, he threw himself into this new work and mastered
it. His work became the model for carved porcelain figures in
Europe. The splendid "snowball vases" covered with innumerable small blooms and figures, the many animals for the

Indian flowers,
Meissen, 1730

Japanese Palace, and the magnificent dining service are all proofs.

Kändler later said that when he entered the factory he "didn't find a single properly made handle." So at the beginning he confined himself to designing important small trimmings without trying any major innovations that would alter the shapes. Only later, with the large services, did he reveal his skills as a sculptor.

Splendid tableware became a medium of gift giving—both for the court and for the nobility. Porcelain became a major part of royal largesse, and in many cases was a portion of the marriage dowries of the princesses.

The crown service for August III, done in 1734, was well proportioned, and the flower painting well designed, but it was in the famous service for Graf Sulkowsky that Kändler's talent was revealed. Unmistakably this was his, the Augsburg gold-and-silversmith work as well as the variations on motifs from the Dresden tower.

Working on the Swan Service for Graf Brühl, who had been overseer of the factory since 1733, Kändler designed in the *Rocaille* style created by Juste-Aurèle Meissonnier, and this became his element. He worked with Johann Friedrich Eberlein on this major project from 1737 until 1741. White swans, intricate fish, shells, flowers, Nereids, sea gods, turkey hens and coats of arms were brought together in a design with new ornaments—the asymmetrical *rocaille*—in carved figures highlighted with gold. This 2,200-piece service, whose power and scope can only be understood when it is all laid out on a long banquet table under the gleam of innumerable candles, had a richness of carved design that was unique, but it was the new rhythmic ground forms that influenced the style of porcelain ware until past the middle of the eighteenth century.

Generally, table service and the small breakfast garnitures, the *"solitaires"* for one person and *"déjeuners"* or *"tête-à-têtes"* for two persons, were kept simple and practical for both court and aristocracy. But the refinement of European table manners in the eighteenth century led to new kinds of vessels, to containers with insets that held heat (or *rechauds*) and coolness;

Indian flowers,
Höchst, 1746

bowls with scalloped rims to hang glasses on; soup tureens and plates and soup bowls with lids. For uncertain hands which trembled easily there was developed the practical "tremble cup" (*trembleuse*), a cup that sat securely in a saucer with a high center rim that kept it from tipping over.

The painters dealt with new motifs in the foreground. The Rococo was the great period for painting on porcelain. Painting in the Chinese style ended by 1735, and, thereafter European motifs were used. Harbor scenes and river landscapes were popular. From Paris came copies of the paintings of Antoine Watteau (1684–1721), which transferred excellently to porcelain. They were not merely painted in several colors, but also in *"camaïeu"* (tone on tone, or painting in different tones of the same color). Meissen preferred green on green, Berlin red on red (iron-red or purple red—*"couleur en rose"*). In 1740, Höroldt painted for Meissen the gold "Watteau" service and in 1745 the green "Watteau" service. Idyllic pastoral scenes, hunting motifs and animals, especially (after engravings by Gottlieb Friedrich Riedel in Ludwigsburg) of minutely detailed fowls, belonged to the great circle of genre paintings so loved in the Rococo period.

For war scenes, themes were taken from the paintings of Rugendas and Wouverman. Flowers were popular, but in a new style. The "Indian flowers" were forgotten. At Meissen the first flowers and insects with shadows were painted (*Saxe ombrée*), then came the "German flowers," already familiar in Vienna. Meadow and garden flowers were soon painted according to patterns, or freely from nature. The scattered flowers, the loose bunches and large bouquets, are among Meissen's most beautiful porcelain decorations.

Underglaze blue decoration was most in demand and the factories produced a great deal, so this porcelain soon became available to the urban middle class. The most famous blue-and-white decoration is certainly the one developed by Meissner in 1739 out of asters, pomegranates, and peaches, the *Zwiebelmuster,* or onion pattern.

When scenes or flower pieces were framed, it was often in the asymmetrical *Rocaille* style of winding trellises or ornamentation in relief which left one side of the scene open.

Typical were surface ornaments like *"mosaiks"* (scales) and trellises in "rocaille" forms, which reached out from the edges into the white surface.

Portrait painting was usually limited to miniatures and the insides of boxes. Less frequently there were large portraits serving as table-pictures. Meissen continued to flourish for a long time. Vienna with its private factory had to struggle against difficulties. With the many newly founded factories even Meissen found itself up against severe competition.

German flowers,
Meissen, 1735

During the Seven Years War (1756–1763) Frederick the Great ordered six services from Meissen, but at the end of the war he himself created out of a private factory in Berlin a Royal Prussian one in which he took a personal interest. At that time Berlin made two extremely beautiful Rococo services

Trellis

Regency ornament, 1730

Surface ornament,
scale pattern

Monogram
(for Mme. Dubarry, Sèvres)

for the Prussian castles and the Breslau state castle, especially
the service made in 1765 in relief ornamentation with espaliers
for the new palace by Friedrich Elias Meyer. This service with
antique ornamentation looks forward to the Louis XVI style.

Bustelli made a large service and small garnitures for
Nymphenburg, and the service for the Einsiedeln Monastery
with painted flowers by Johannes Daffinger is a brilliant
achievement from the Zurich manufacturers.

Sèvres freed itself early from the Meissen influence and
developed simple, smooth forms which were made from the
soft paste or artificial porcelain. Wonderfully colored backgrounds, under which was the rare *"bleu mourant"* found in
Berlin two years before the death of Frederick the Great, or

Relief ornament, Berlin

Antique ornament, Berlin

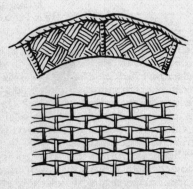

Ozier pattern;
basketweave

patterns such as the animal-like *"oeil-de-perdrix"* (literally, partridge eyes) combined with brilliant colors, are typical of Sèvres ware of this period, but it was often, unfortunately, very fragile.

An important stoneware producer should be mentioned here, Josiah Wedgwood of Staffordshire, England. High quality and the high prices it brought made his work influential on the porcelain of the following period.

By the middle of the eighteenth century there was a reaction against the frivolous Rococo and its swirling modes of expression. It was now beginning to seem tasteless.

Sèvres *"oeil-de-perdrix"*
(Background decoration)

The ideas of Jean-Jacques Rousseau (1712–1778), his call for a return to nature and simplicity and his rejection of royal absolutism, as well as Johann Joachim Winckelmann's rediscovery of the ancient world, produced during the reign of Louis XVI a gradual change in style that appeared as a tendency toward linear precision. The transition was not complete: Rococo forms were found side by side with early classical ones, and many lovers of the Rococo continued to hold out until well into classicism. But in any case there was a shift to more precise forms. Instead of the happy, loose, asymmetrical *rocaille* in relief, or scenes on the edge, the painters offered round or oval closed wreaths formed of flowers, leaves, and twigs, sometimes bound with a streamer. Flowers were used with monograms and garlands.

The trend toward simplicity changed genre painting. Cavaliers and their ladies gave way to peasants, and instead of hunting scenes there were cattle. In Berlin in 1771 scenes were painted on a *solitaire* (table service for one) from Lessing's *Minna von Barnhelm* in the style of illustrations by David Chodowiecki. Later Meissen used scenes from Goethe's *Werther,* painted by David Schubert.

By 1800 the fashion was for Empire, the representative style of Napoleon. Form and color were increasingly restrained. The tone-on-tone painting appeared now in gray *(grisaille)*. Portraits shrank to silhouettes, the master of which was the Berlin painter Wilhelm Dittmar.

The most effective examples of the period are the large-scale Pearl Service of Domenicus Auliczek, made in Nymphenburg for the Bavarian court, in white, blue, and gold with carved pearl necklaces on every vessel and every plate; and the painted medallions with *grisaille* landscape painting by Paul Boehngen.

Berlin created services that derived from English silver and Wedgwood models.

Scenes were enclosed, not with flowers, but with a rectangular gold band, and the flower garlands became garlands of laurel and oak.

The growth of scientific knowledge led paradoxically to a narrowing of artistic fantasy. The Flora Danica service from Copenhagen for Catherine the Great of Russia is an example of the interest in flower paintings in accurate botanical style. On the advice of the botanist Theador Holmskjöld, a student of the natural scientist Linne, the Nurenberg flower painter, Johann Christoph Bayer, followed the colorful copper etchings of Danish flora, *Flora Danica* of Christian Öders (1790–1802). Each piece of the service carried on its underside the Latin name for every pictured plant.

However, there were livelier flowers on porcelain. In Berlin, Johann Friedrich Schulz painted his flowers *en terrasse,* that is, beginning from under the base of the vessel, flowers grew upward to different heights. Somewhat later, in Empire and Biedermeier styles symbolic flowers appeared. For instance, the initial letters of several flowers bound together to form a wreath could spell the name of a young lady. There were charming picture riddles on the cups like "Turn to the roses and forget me not." Roses and forget-me-nots were painted between the words.

Ideal landscapes were a thing of the past. Instead, there were urban and rural pictures that were true to nature. Especially fine were views of Berlin and Potsdam on splendid vases, dishes, and cups. The cups, particularly Biedermeier styles, became important as collectors' items. This enthusiasm came from England where visitors to some business firms were given cups. The decorations were full of fantasy. Some people sent remembrance cups with their own silhouettes on them, which could be ordered at the factory. Although coffee drinking had become a custom among all classes, these cups were usually not used but rather displayed in glass cases.

The finds at Herculaneum and Pompeii exercised great influence on the form and decoration of porcelain from about 1780. People were enchanted with the ancient ceramic forms, and imitated them. The wonderful frescos excited the painters.

Vienna had two notable painters: George Perl, master of a gold relief technique developed at Sèvres; and Joseph Leithner, the color specialist, who discovered new colors like those of the ancient archeological models—dark and light violet,

Flora Danica
decoration, 1790

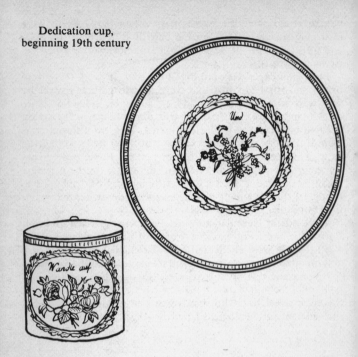

Dedication cup,
beginning 19th century

copper-red luminous grounds, and the Leithner blue named after him.

Unfortunately, often the over-rich painting and gilding vulgarized the porcelain.

Along with the Berlin "Field Marshal" service that Friedrich Wilhelm III commissioned in 1820 for Willington von Schadow, the tureens for which are surely more *pièces d' occasion* than for soup, there are two astonishingly beautiful creations by Johann Peter Melchior, who after 1798 was the successor to Auliczek in Nymphenburg: the elegant White Empire Service with wide gold edges and gold "pine cones" as lid handles (after 1800); and a tea service (1820) in white and gold that was named Shield after the raised base of the teapot.

Cup with silhouette

Nymphenburg 1810

THE HAUSMALER

There was a group of porcelain painters who were not employed by a factory but worked for themselves at home, the so-called *hausmaler* (literally, house painters). Some of their work is valued today, but they were often called botchers and bunglers —in some cases with justification, for not every *hausmaler* was talented. Meissen and Vienna had plenty of trouble with the painters who worked at home, for they bought quality white porcelain and sold it painted, not always painted well. There were exceptional *hausmaler* who had experience of fired painting through their work with faience, glass painting, and metal decoration at Augsburg, Breslau, and Bayreuth. But at Meissen until 1717 everything was still painted cold with lacquer and gold leaf.

The Augsburger Johannes Auffenwerth worked early with black, iron red, a green, and a purple-violet as well as with gold and silver. He secured a steady supply of white porcelain from Meissen to paint until he had improved his own factory's work technically and artistically and could rely on his employees. After his death in 1728 his workshop, which he had operated with his daughter, closed.

In 1729 Meissen forbade the sale of white porcelain, but it continued secretly, and in the fair stalls even the waste, the *brack,* was sold.

Among the best known of the *hausmaler* was von Auffenwerth, who from 1715 to 1725, painted interiors, country scenes based on pictures by Watteau, and chinoiserie. All of this influenced the styles at Meissen, where Höroldt developed the small gold and vividly colored Chinese figures into his own inimitable style.

Ignaz Bottengruber from Breslau was another important *hausmaler*. He worked for the Viennese manufacturers. His most notable decorations were lively mythological scenes, thick crowds of bacchantes, war scenes, and hunting pictures in vivid colors. Besides these, he did rich decorations with vine leaves and ribbons, a type of ornament that had been popular in Vienna since the Regency.

In Breslau his student Carl Ferdinand worked with two talented black-enamel painters, David and Ignaz Preussler.

Black enamel painting (*schwarzlot*) was a typical *hausmaler* technique. Developed originally in the Middle Ages for painting church windows, it was used in the second half of the seventeenth century, especially in Nurenburg for faience painting. This painting, brown to black, often built up with gold, was often applied to Chinese porcelain, white, blue and white or even colored. There is a dish in which a straw-covered European peasant house painted in black enamel is set in a Chinese landscape. Sometimes only leaf work and some gold was added to make a decoration "European."

Böhmen in 1720 created a combination of the black painting with iron red.

Grapevine pattern in underglaze chrome green,
Meissen 1817

Section of a
battle painting
(1768–1774)

Meissen took over the painting with black enamel from Auffenwerth; Vienna from Bottengruber. In Vienna it was particularly cultivated by du Paquier. In 1740 in Vienna, Jacob Helchis used a quill pen for the first time instead of a brush and made delicately outlined drawings that looked like copper engravings.

From 1760 Meissen had incised its waste porcelain with a special mark as an identifying sign, thereby hoping to stop the painters who worked outside the factory, but used the Meissen product. But some continued, nonetheless. Fine paintings based on engravings by Nilson appeared between 1745 and 1765, done by Franz Ferdinand Mayer from Bohemia on Meissen pieces. And in Bayreuth in 1740, Johann Friedrich Metzsch and Johann Christoph Jucht painted on porcelain acquired from Meissen. Jucht had a good eye for color, and the painting had genuine quality.

However, toward the end of the eighteenth century the *hausmaler* lost their importance and they dwindled in number. The manufacturers had improved their techniques so that they could sell at good prices, and there were so many manufacturers that the "house painters" could no longer provide competition. The ban on selling white porcelain was finally lifted in 1800.

Porcelain painting was enthusiastically taken up by rich amateurs. Aristocratic ladies proved themselves successful at this work. In England it was a favorite hobby to paint a complete service and then have it baked in a factory. Goethe sent Frau von Stein a cup that he had painted himself.

The case of Canon August Otto Ernst von dem Busch was somewhat special. He used diamonds for cutting into the ceramic surface, and used lampblack to create landscapes embellished with ruins.

KNICKKNACKERY

The *galanterien* (knickknackery) of the eighteenth century comprise an especially appealing aspect of porcelain. These were small utility and luxury items shaped and painted with extreme care.

There were enormous numbers of boxes—round, oval, and four-cornered—which, for the most part, were used as snuff boxes. The prices that have come down to us show how highly this artistic work was valued. Painted inside and out with flowers, fruits, landscapes, and figures—and combinations, too, like fruit on the outside and landscapes inside—they are often genuine works of art. In royal circles there was an unbridled passion for these small luxury items. The small porcelain boxes had pride of place, since they could be individually painted with portraits, or with dedications or coats of arms on the insides of the lids, and could be given away as special gifts.

Hardly less popular were pipe bowls which were shaped like heads. Womens' heads were the most popular, but there were also Hussars, Poles, and Turks. For pipe smokers a pipe cleaner is indispensable, and so there were charming containers called *"Jungfernbeinchen"* (maidens' limbs), which in Biedermeier style often received a finishing touch in the form of a flea.

A mark of the cavalier was a walking stick with a knob. In addition to painted porcelain knobs, there were magically modelled little heads, small masterpieces by great artists. Gentlemen wore porcelain buttons. There were many more

small items for ladies: earrings, sewing paraphernalia like
thimbles and needle boxes, sponge boxes for sponges dipped in
perfume, cases for small instruments, watch cases, table clocks,
and all the many items for the dressing table. Scent bottles were
much loved. Meissen made small bottles in the form of figures,
and those made by the English manufacturer Chelsea became
famous. They are rich in imaginative invention and charm.
There was no contemporary motif in figure carving that didn't
turn up as a "Chelsea toy."

Scent bottle from Chelsea
(England);
"Chelsea toy," 1765

ILLUSTRATED SUMMARY OF CHANGES IN STYLE IN THE EIGHTEENTH CENTURY

Baroque: Simple forms, versions either of Chinese models or of models by gold- and silversmiths.

Painting: "Indian flowers" and chinoiserie in gold and in color.

In Meissen, wonderful ground colors in reserve and flower painting. Ornamental borders: hanging patterns, gold-tipped patterns (Meissen), Vines and ribbons (Vienna). The shift to Rococo was established through Kändler's Swan Service. Restless baroque forms, the take-over of *rocaille* as carved and painted element.

Painting: The Chinese patterns gradually disappear.

Rococo: The forms developed by Kändler were refined rather than abandoned.

Painting: This was the great period of porcelain painting! European motifs were much used—harbor scenes, landscapes, Watteau scenes, "tone on tone" *(camaïeu),* shepherd scenes, war and hunting pictures, animals (fowl), flowers ("German" instead of "Indian"; at first flowers with shadows, then flowers strewn about, and large loose bouquets).

Miniature portraits on boxes. Ornamental borders: asymmetrical *rocailles* in relief (relief ornamentation) combined with painting, trellises (swinging espaliers open on one side). Surface ornamentation: *"mosaiks"* (scale patterns), and lattice work.

The transition to Classicism (Louis XVI) brought stricter forms; instead of *rocaille* as a framing device, closed wreaths of flowers and leaves.

Painting: Change in genre painting toward the rustic. Instead of shepherd scenes, peasant ones; bucolic scenes instead of hunting pictures. Flowers as monograms, or wound into garlands, often with bows. Turkey hens and mythological themes.

Scenes from *Minna von Barnhelm* and *Werther* on porcelain. Ruins and English parkland scenes.

Classicism/Empire: Smooth, straight, cool forms, dependence upon antique models like amphora, urns, kraters and ornaments.

Painting: Imitations of items discovered in Pompeii and Herculaneum: frescos, gray-on-gray *(grisaille)* painting, portrait-silhouettes, war scenes, flowers in botanical exactitude, flowers *"en terrasse,"* symbolic flowers, flower patterns as a ground.

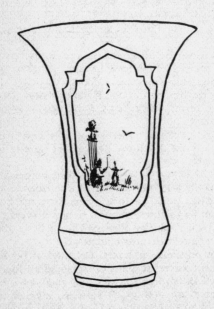

Vase from Meissen
with Chinese figures in reserve (1730–1735)

Teapot by Meissen, 1720

Meissen, 1730

Picture borders as four-cornered gold frames. Colored rocks and minerals, often over-richly painted and gilded, imitation of Chinese lacquer work (Vienna).

Meissen, small pitcher, 1736

Vienna 1719 (du Paquier).
The original of this cup
bears the inscription:
"Honor to God alone."

Potpourri vase,
Fürstenberg, 1765.
These covered vases, often
profusely perforated, were filled
with lavender, rose petals, etc.

Coffee pot, milk pitcher,
and cup from Fürstenberg, 1760–1765

A pitcher of 1766
with the decorative design
"New Ornament," developed in
Berlin along with "Antique
Ornament" and "Relief Ornament"

Pitcher from Ludwigsburg,
1770—1775

Pitcher from Berlin, 1780

Coffee pot, Berlin, 1782

Teapot from Sèvres, 1760

Teapot with a
grotesque mask
on the bottom of
the spout. Berlin,
Gotzkowski period, 1763

The severe form of
a teapot from Vienna, 1780

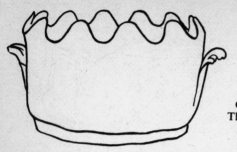

Glass cooler, 1770.
The glasses were hung
by the foot on the
scalloped edge.

Covered cup,
here a *trembleuse*,
1780, Fürstenberg

Trembleuse, Vienna, 1760

Cup shapes from Berlin, 1790–1815

Tureen from the time of du Paquier,
Vienna, 1730–1740

Meissen, 1735–1740;
Tureen from the service of Elector Philipp Carl of Mainz,
from a mold by Kändler

Meissen, 1738;
modeled by Kändler for Elector Clemens August of Köln

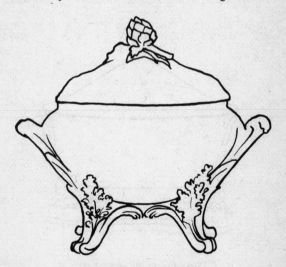

Tureen from a Sèvres service,
1759

Tureen from a Pearl Service
by Auliczek, Nymphenburg, 1792–1795

Tureen from the service of
Field Marshal von Schadow, Berlin, 1820

Vase by Sèvres

Bohemian vase (1839)

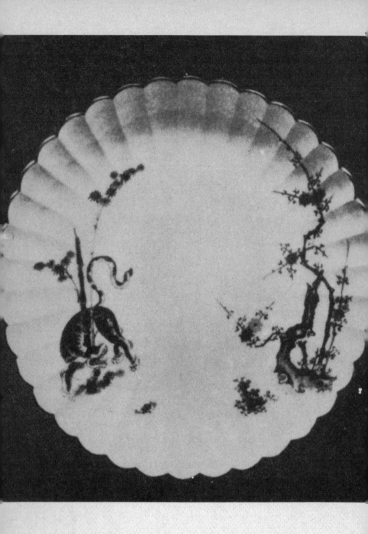

Plate in flower form with overglaze painting
in the manner of Kakiemon, Arita, Japan

Above: Meissen, 1715. Polished jar (Böttger stoneware)

Top left: Meissen. Teapot in "Höroldt Chinese" style, 1725

Above: Meissen, 1715. Porcelain ware with Chinese painting

Above: Meissen, 1715. Bottle of Böttger porcelain

Above: Meissen. Vase with "Indian flowers," Höroldt painting, 1730–1735

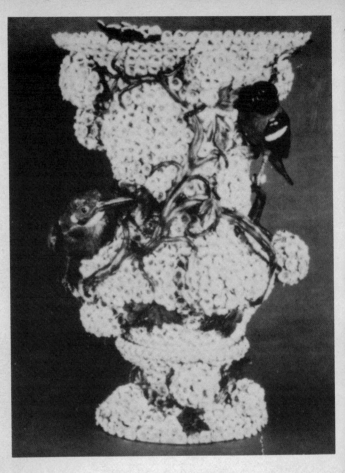

Above: Meissen. "Snowball" vase with birds, 1740

Tureen from the famous Swan Service by Johann Joachim Kändler, Meissen, 1737–1741. This multi-legged tureen harks back to the old table settings made of pastry and sweets which were set up as *schauessen,* food to be looked at. The court pastry cook, Lachapelle, is said to have acted as consultant to Kändler on this project.

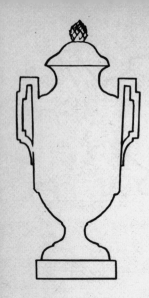

Fürstenberg,
end of 18th century

Nymphenburg, 1821

Teapot from Berlin, ca. 1818

PORCELAIN FIGURES
OF THE EIGHTEENTH CENTURY

The renowned archaeologist Johann Joachim Winckelmann (1717–1768) called the small varicolored porcelain figures, which we now consider the high point of European porcelain, "ludicrous puppets." Aside from their aesthetic value—they are often the smallest yet the most famous works of their creators—they give an interesting and lighthearted picture of courtly and middle-class life in the eighteenth century. Deep sorrow and pain are absent in porcelain, but many contemporary themes are often depicted affectionately.

Quite early (1715–1720) excellent figures from Italian comedy *(commedia dell'arte)* were modeled by Böttger at Meissen as well as dwarfish forms based on the work of the French painter Jacques Callot (1592–1635). Then in 1731 Johann Joachim Kändler in Meissen came up with a further development in the porcelain art. The king and the artist, both temperamentally inclined toward the baroque, actually inspired one another and lent each other support. This happy arrangement, for the the king's Japanese Palace show (it was in August 1697), resulted in figures larger than life size of apostles and saints, as well as animals. There were vases and a remarkably successful glockenspiel.

Kändler's predecessor, Gottlieb Kirchner, after working in partnership for two years, left the manufactory in 1733. That same year the king died.

Kändler had enormous creative ability. He overcame the

Exotic beast of prey for the Japanese Palace; mold by Johann Gottlieb Kirchner, ca. 1730

difficulties the medium of porcelain presented, especially working in large figures. Under his hands many figures, groups, and animals were created that became a standard of excellence for the eighteenth century. His animals are among the best of Meissen. For this we have to thank the king's passion for domestic and foreign animals, which he kept on his estate, as well as his passion for porcelain. The animals for the Japanese Palace had to be created life size. The king had wild animal preserves, fish ponds, and hunt scenes as well as domestic and exotic creatures, which the artists studied and learned from.

Earlier, Kirchner had begun to make large, white, somewhat rigid and bizarre animals for the Japanese Palace, at the time Kändler came to Meissen. Until Kirchner's departure, despite tensions, they worked together. Kändler finally finished the animals for the Japanese Palace. Ultimately it was his wonderfully painted representations of birds and savage and wild beasts that set the standard for all European animal ceramics.

Porcelain artists in the eighteenth century felt a natural affinity and sympathy toward China. In the beginning they imitated Kuan Yin goddesses and the small, squat incense burners (in Europe often falsely called pagodas). This Chinese influence was felt in all areas of the arts and trade crafts; furniture was bejeweled with inlaid work and lacquer; porcelain painting and figures were created in this mode. Kändler in Meissen created an exquisite Chinese group, Bustelli at Nymphenburg made figures and von Lück and Melchior made admirable groups at Frankenthal, Höchst and Ludwigsburg. However, slowly and surely they became more and more Europeanized. The last good Chinese group was created by Elias Meyer in Berlin, after which the Chinese figure virtually disappeared.

Besides the Chinese, the Turk in fantastic garb was very popular. Sometimes he had a European face, and it became rather a popular game to guess which member of royalty was camouflaged in the costume of the Turk.

Court people at that time loved to get dressed up as simple folk and, dressed as a shepherd or shepherdess, play coquettish and frivolous games. One could never be quite sure if the pretty shepherdess, farmer, fisher, gardener, or musician wasn't per-

Actor from Capodimonte (Italian) ca. 1750

haps a member of society. All the maufactories reflected this free and easy cheerfulness and they presented this charming frivolity of the time in their shepherd scenes.

The intimate contact between artist and court in the eighteenth century helps to explain the artist's sympathy with courtly life. Elegantly and tastefully the artists depicted piquant love stories, slight anecdotes and gallant adventures in porcelain. Several couples and single figures, cavaliers and their ladies, as well as pages and ladies' maids, could be combined in one large scene.

There were also sympathetic representations of burghers and tradespeople, and soldiers, mendicants, merchants, and town criers in porcelain. And more and more, there were children, city and country children, and children as allegorical figures and *putti* and cupids.

These small figures were only rarely thought of as portraits. The portrait was reserved for the bust or the relief medal. These were almost always in white with small colored embellishments such as a medal or decoration on the base. Occasionally there were representations of noted figures on horseback or free standing. Toward the end of the eighteenth century these were frequently done entirely in white unglazed biscuit porcelain.

Nymphenburg created for the court, which was so fond of hunting porcelain dishes decorated with scenes of the "Great Green Hunt," the "Small Yellow Hunt," and based on these, Bustelli's "Nymphenburg Hunt." Of this beautiful genre we should mention Lanz's small "Halili Group" and von Lück's large "The Hunter from Kurpfalz," both Frankenthaler, as well as the delicate "Duckshooting Pair" of Melchior at Höchst.

The Thüringian manufactories scarcely dealt with the hunt motif since they had a solidly burgher clientele, and the hunt was a pastime of the nobility.

One of the most beautiful and inexhaustible subjects was the theater, and there was hardly a manufactory which didn't create figures based on the characters of Italian comedy (*commedia dell'arte*). Meissen brought out the first comedy figures in 1715 in Böttger stoneware, and from then on artists created increasing numbers.

The Italian extemporaneous comedy inspired every painter

and sculptor. Of this the absolute high point is represented by the eight pairs that Bustelli created for Nymphenburg—lively, extremely lifelike and elegant models probably influenced by the Bavarian wood sculptor Ignaz Günther.

Around 1770 Italian comedy started losing its popularity, replaced, till the end of the century, by figures from the French theater. Figures from the ancient world or mythology were popular, too, and like the characters of the French opera, they were created in typical French Baroque costumes. The ancient heroes appeared with perukes and feather-crowned helmets and boots. However, these costumes were dealt with handsomely.

The lavishly designed world of the ballet was illustrated in porcelain too. The famous ballerinas, Camaro and Sallé, were portrayed by Frankenthal; the Ludwigsburg manufactory, in 1763, sculpted an entire ballet in the form of a centerpiece with the title "Neptune's Basin" for Duke Carl Eugen von Württemburg.

Music also was a source of ideas. The Fürstenburg musicians are exquisite, and the now lost Ludwigsburg Soloists which Beyer made in 1765 were famous. Kändler created a delicate scene at the spinet and Bustelli made a woman playing a xylophone disturbing a sleeper. All the manufactories created lovely, often amusing, figures and groups playing all kinds of instruments. The most original by far is the one made by Kändler and Reinecke at Meissen of an ape band dressed in long perukes and courtly clothes. This was copied by Rombrich in Fürstenburg.

Mythological subjects played an increasingly larger part in the production of the manufactories. Artists and the rising middle class were familiar with the ancient gods and heroes and the works of the classical poets. Winckelmann's excavations and his writings on classical art stirred an interest in the classical age.

From around 1750 to 1760 Kändler at Meissen created "Mount Parnassus," a large group with Apollo, Pegasus, and the nine muses. Around 1770 Konrad Linck at Frankenthal produced some of his finest work, with scenes like "Meleager and Atalanta," "Okeanos and Thetis," and "Paris and Helen."

These mythological subjects were later turned out in biscuit porcelain which corresponded nicely in their cool unglazed white to Winckelmann's ideal of a "noble innocence and a still greatness." Sometimes these subjects were rather ponderous, but this reflected the tone of the time. There was much interest in allegorical figures. Even the most charming and interesting creations seem too encoded and cryptic, today. Representations of the elements, and the seasons of the year, the continents, the liberal arts, the five senses, or the twelve months and Love are for the most part relatively easy to divine. For example, winter is represented by a charming figure of a woman with a muff. Autumn has a basket of fruit as a characteristic. Linck in Frankenthal symbolized the four seasons in small portrait busts. America is sometimes represented as a gaily colored Indian with an alligator; Europa sometimes is riding a bull, and Africa is often shown as a baroque black prince. A figure with blueprints in his hand, perhaps standing next to the capital of a column might indeed be an architect. In contrast, there are abstract allegories, such as the conclusion of peace, or treaties, that are tough to understand.

Figures from Italian Comedy (Commedia dell' Arte) Designed According to Molds by Anton Bustelli

Bustelli's figures from the popular theater from which *commedia dell'arte* sprang are rendered with such courtly grace that one can assume they were based on actual noble models.

The old Italian comedy actors excited the spectator through lively performances, contemporary satire, a ready wit, both tasteful and tasteless jokes, and an incomparable sense of mimicry. The recognizable types always appeared in character masks.

Pantalone is a somewhat mischievous old man with a pointed nose and beard. Though he is greedy, he holds his hands behind him under a long black cape. He always wear red trousers.

Harlequin is often his servant.

Harlequin (Arlecchino) wears tight-fitting patchwork pants. He is the oldest comedy figure. He is a mischief maker and calls to mind a clown. Women find him irresistible but he's not in the heroic mold—he'd rather have a good meal.

Scaramouche first appeared in the seventeenth century, in Naples. He is a touching comic figure. He influenced Molière and was much loved in France. He is dressed mostly in black.

Mezzetin was originally the theatrical name for a comic who made a cutting remark about Louis XIV and was greatly disliked.

Pulcinella, originally from Naples, is the prototype for the German Hanswurst and the English Punch. His origins are in pre-Roman times. He is garbed in a loose white smock with a ruff around his neck, white pants, and a pointed hat. He is also shown with a paunch and a hump.

Brighella comes from France. He is an intriguer.

Pierrot (Pedrolino, Giglio, Gilles), also French, is the dumb servant.

Mezzetin, Scaramouche and Harlequin were often servants to the aristocracy.

Octavio is always a languishing lover.

There were fewer stage roles for women, and instead of the standardized costumes often worn by the men, they wore fashionable dress or fantastic attire. Usually their appearance depended on their fancy and their taste.

Pantalone

Julia

Capitano

Scaramouche

Leda

Pierrot

Columbine

Donna Martina

Dottore

MAJOR CHANGES IN STYLE IN PORCELAIN FIGURES IN THE EIGHTEENTH CENTURY

Baroque figures are cannily and expressively modelled to seem animated. They stem from the earlier tradition of the grotesque figures of Callot and the comedy figures of Böttger stoneware at Meissen, the great apostle figures and the life-size animals in white-glazed porcelain that Kändler and Kirchner made for the Japanese Palace.

At this time Chinese figures were modelled on authentic Chinese models. The Chinese were discovered by European artists and quickly adapted. The pedestals for the figures were plain, round or oval, sometimes decorated with flowers.

Somewhat before 1740, Kändler was already making the transition to the Rococo. He refined his figures and painted them with beautiful, strong colors. The woman's dress was often embellished with blossoms.

In the Rococo style, figures are more delicate. Soft, embossed flowers were used. Black was used only where absolutely necessary, such as on shoes, buckles or hats. The skin was a creamy white, but red was applied to the lips, the cheeks, the eyelids and even the nostrils. The bases were also modified. At first there appeared small ceramic *rocaille* on the surface; ultimately they did the entire base in *rocaille* which was carried lightly and clearly right up to the decoration in the scene. Bustelli was a master of this.

The high point of Rococo is the shell form in *rocaille*.

Between 1760 and 1770 there was a transition to neo-

German tinted flower (*Saxe ombrée*);
Meissen, 1740

classicism, under French influence. The great representative of
this style was Konrad Linck at Frankenthal. His elegant figures
with delicate faces were finely painted, with strong lines; the
skin had a rosy glow. Bases took on a regular rectangular shape.
Melchior at Höchst typically dealt with these as just rock bases.
The strong influence of the French style made great advances
in neoclassicism when around the middle of the century Sèvres
developed a biscuit porcelain which corresponded to ancient
marble models. Many statues by old masters were executed in
miniature in biscuit porcelain.

The small ceramics in color dealt more with scenes of country and burgher life. The colors became stronger and darker,
the designs less subtle. The tradition of small figures remained
strong up to Biedermeier, around the middle of the nineteenth
century.

THE NINETEENTH CENTURY AND ART NOUVEAU, 1895–1910

In the eighteenth century porcelain was a strong artistic expression of its time. It was one of the great means of representing contemporary princely figures, and until neoclassicism became the vogue, form and decoration were unified in intent. But toward the end of the century fascination with porcelain waned. The means of production were no longer secret, and the artists degraded porcelain to the function of background decoration. Many subjects created in porcelain were transferred to oil paintings, and by the turn of the century the abundant and splendid decoration had been reduced to a level where it scarcely had any validity. The lifelike warmth of figures like Kändler's or Bustelli's had been lost.

The Napoleonic wars had left Europe poor and the manufactories suffered economic difficulties. Manufactories that had previously been dependent on royal subsidies went out of business in the beginning of the nineteenth century. The social upheaval of the time demanded other modes of business operation.

In the course of the century the manufactories at Fürstenberg and Nymphenburg were leased into private hands; other manufactories struggled along against the competition of English stoneware, from 1812 (the breakup of the continental system) until around the middle of the century, the time of England's supremacy in the marketplace. The transfer process, which was patented in Liverpool in 1752 and eventually was to cause the death of traditional porcelain painting, was introduced in Berlin in 1810, and in 1814 at Meissen. Around this time Meissen started its series of Etruscan reliefs, typical of Wedgwood jasper ware, as decoration on its porcelain.

The establishment of the tariff union in 1828 and finally the abolition of the inland duty in 1834 helped to ease the competition and afforded some free trade.

In 1814 Carl Magnus Huntschenreuther, a former porcelain painter at Wallendorf in Hohenberg, founded a factory with his son on the Eger River, in Bavaria, which still exists as a large-scale enterprise. The factory, however, is more characterized by good management than artistic achievement.

As for artistic development in this period of shifting styles, Philip Rosenthal stands out. His factory was started in 1867 in Selb and from the beginning it was outstanding. It is today one of the great German porcelain factories.

The nineteenth century was characterized by insecurity in all artistic areas and a disorganized search for new solutions until the last decade of the century when Art Nouveau developed.

Earlier in the century, the old styles came in for a revival. Imitations of ancient forms had not been successful in the

Zwiebelmuster (onion pattern) border

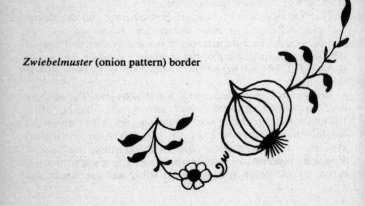

beginning of the century, nor was an attempt around the middle of the century to bring about a "second Rococo," so the designers went back to the eighteenth century and before. There was a revival of Renaissance designs, imitations of Italian faience, Delft Baroque faience, and German clay tankards.

There was little room for porcelain in the overstuffed, plush dark rooms of the middle of the century, except for blue-and-white Meissen onion pattern and similar blue-and-white decorations. These were much loved as dinner services.

Experts have subdivided this period's styles into "neo-Renaissance," "neo-Gothic," and "neo-Baroque." The first World Exposition in Paris in 1851 pointed up with merciless insight the artistic inadequacy of expression of these styles. Though competently executed, all this seemed hopeless compared to works of real artistic merit.

In England, artists had been rebelling against industrialization for some time. William Morris argued vociferously for a return to handcrafts and the patterns of the Middle Ages. His views about the totality of art, along with the reform thinking of John Ruskin, were what eventually led to Art Nouveau.

Prince Albert commissioned the German architect and art theoretician Gottfried Semper to develop a program of reform. Also in Berlin, in accord with Semper's thought, they set up a commission to improve the level of achievement and the general quality of porcelain.

Around this time the Victoria and Albert Museum was founded.

The London international exhibition of 1862 saw the first success of new design ideas along these lines in the applied arts.

Meanwhile, in 1854, the American Commodore Perry had succeeded in opening Japanese harbors to trade. In 1856 the first Japanese woodcuts appeared in Paris and caused a sensation among the Impressionist painters. Once again it was the Far East that showed the way to a new artistic innovation.

The artistic potters recognized the beauty of the seemingly spontaneous glazing of the Japanese and Chinese techniques. Their eyes were opened, their feelings educated by the possibilities now open to them through the aid of these techniques. Gradually there was experimentation everywhere, especially in the small ateliers.

In all the great circles of porcelain laboratories, Sèvres, Copenhagen, and Berlin, they succeeded in producing the wonderful Chinese ground colors, *sang de boeuf*, celadon, powder blue.

The great pioneer was Jean Carriès who was especially successful in uniting forms and stoneware glazes; Adolphe Clément in Copenhagen and Berlin, and the porcelain chemist Hermann Seger who developed a soft porcelain around 1880, based on Japanese models whose complicated glazes were made to comply with metal glazing sensitive to heat. It was also discovered by chance that with careful handling and with a crystalline glaze of an alloy of zinc and titanium they could be extraordinarily effective in baking in embossed colors.

A new mode of underglazing was developed for painting the porcelain. Meissen in 1817 for cobalt blue had developed a chrome oxidized green (Meissen "vine leaf"). In the eighties they developed further green, brown, and red tones. The ideas were only limited by the fact that the china still had to be functional, and to satisfy a wide range of buyers.

In 1903 Henry van de Velde created for Meissen a simple tea service in a greatly streamlined form with an ornamental gold decor. Nymphenburg brought out a service by Levallois; Berlin had an undulating-wave-patterned service, a fan-shaped service, and the significant designs of Theo Schmuz-Baudiss, "Ceres" and "Pensée." Alf Wallander in Rörstrand developed a tea service in underglaze blue with shallow flower relief around 1900.

Vases permitted more freedom. The ancient and Asian proportions and forms were altered. A new relationship was evolved between flowers and their containers. Painters and ceramic decorators preferred unusual or bizarre flowers like the iris, the orchid, or the clematis, as well as creating ornamentation from the until then ignored parts of plants such as the stems and leaves.

The American, David Haviland, in Limoges had created an entirely new and un-French kind of decoration by 1870. His motifs of grass, seaweed, conches, and shrimp were used and further developed by other painters. Human figures appeared mostly in symbolic guise: mermaids were common, but there were also dancing women in abbreviated costumes. Sèvres brought out a pattern like that.

The state manufactories trained many splendid porcelain painters. Sèvres refined the technique of layered relief painting (*pâte-sur-pâte*) based on Chinese forms. The layers of porcelain clays produced excellent representations in relief, against which the deeply colored background shone through.

The most important development in decor came from Copenhagen. In 1882 Philip Schou purchased the manufactory, and in 1885 he named the painter Arnold Krog (1856–1931) artistic director. That year they took a research trip together through England, Holland, Belgium, and France. Krog was inspired by his Japanese-influenced Parisian friends and developed a painting style that greatly influenced all European manufactories.

In 1889 Copenhagen won the Grand Prix d'Honneur at the Paris World Exposition. By 1900 Berlin, Meissen, and St. Petersburg had changed over to the Copenhagen style. Alf Wallander at the Swedish manufactory in Rörstrand was also inspired by the style.

Besides Japanese motifs, Krog favored motifs of home, landscape, animals, and flowers. The chemist Adolphe Clément had created what was a technical prerequisite for Krog's impressive painting, a hard blue tone that permitted the convex surface of the porcelain to be delicately embellished.

For Berlin, Theo Schmuz-Baudiss painted landscapes and city scenes in hard underglazes such as green, gray, and rose. Above all, we should mention his somber mood pieces such as "Autumn," "Blue Hour," and "Berlin Evening." Under his directorship in 1900 Art Nouveau came to Berlin. Along with him, Adolph Flad and Heinrich Lang painted abstracts in gold and in sharp fiery colors.

At this time Nymphenburg produced the popular landscapes and animals of Rudolf Siek and the flora works of Adalbert Niemeyer.

In the nineteenth century there were scarcely any new developments in sculpture. Lighthearted figures, heroic scenes, and sentimental guardian angels for children predominated. However, we should mention the molds of Gottfried Schadow and Hans Christian Genelli for the Berlin manufactory and the portrait busts of Christian Rauch, made around 1840.

Around 1860 there was a revival of the Rococo, but without rekindling the spirit of that time. The artists searched all territories. Then from Copenhagen came the outstanding animal sculptures of C. Thomsen (cats), C.F. Liisberg, and C. Nielsen.

Sèvres created the unremarkable centerpiece group *"Le jeu de l'écharpe,"* made by Agathon Leonard (1900), a group of dancing women wrapped in pleated robes. About this time dance made its mark on the art of porcelain. With the beginning of expressive modern dance, which overshadowed the classic ballet, great female dancers became public figures. The famous Isadora Duncan's "Serpent Dance" with its long colored veils, Loie Fuller, Ruth St. Denis and Sent M'ahesa inspired artists, especially Fuller with her body enswathed in waving veils—all appeared in porcelain. In Berlin Hubatsch modeled Ruth St. Denis, and Rosenthal created Sent M'ahesa.

A famous work of Adolf Amberg (Berlin, 1905) is his outstanding "Bridal Procession." Josef Wackerle created in Nymphenburg remarkable works such as the "Woman with Muff," and the "Woman in Striped Taffeta."

From 1906 to 1913 Ernst Barlach worked for the Schwarzburg mold workshop, a quite special little entity. His great motif was figures of Russian farmers and beggars. As his last work he created the portrait bust of the actress Tilla Durieux, the wife of his publisher and friend Paul Cassirer.

Alongside the Copenhagen animals one can place those of Paul Esser and Richard Gaul for Meissen and those of Julius Feldmann and Edmundt Otto for Berlin. They were painted in underglaze colors and their bases were highly decorated.

Paul Scheurich first worked in porcelain sculpture in 1912, and his "The Woman and the Hind" in the best sense harks back to Rococo. He worked for Berlin and Meissen.

The reign of Art Nouveau was very short. In 1895 Samuel Bing arranged the first Art Nouveau exposition in Paris. Though it was a total flop, two years later he was enthusiastically taken up in Dresden. Henry van de Velde, a native of Belgium was one of the most famous and versatile Art Nouveau artists. He settled in Germany and put together in Weimar an arts and crafts institute where he worked until 1914.

In 1907 in Munich a cooperative of fifteen factory owners

and fifteen artists was founded, the "German Workers' Federation," as a reaction against the purely decorative Art Nouveau, in favor of a new realism. By 1910 there was a cooperative in Austria and in 1913 one in Sweden.

Many objects which we today call Art Nouveau were actually executed before or after the short time it flourished, and the precise time boundaries are difficult to set. Many forms we think of today as modern actually had their origin then.

Despite many great and interesting achievements, Art Nouveau is often looked down upon because not only was there industrial exploitation of the market, so that it was inundated with less than the best, but also an oversophistication set in because the artists were pressured to constantly come up with something new. Today we are much better able to judge the really convincing works of the style.

Art Nouveau in porcelain was characterized by interesting and wonderful glazing, and a unity of form and decor. Its inspiration came in great part from Japan. Its surface painting, its sculptural and painterly motifs were from nature, though often with stylized ornamentation. "The line is a force," van de Velde said.

Seger porcelain,
Berlin, ca. 1890

A vase in the form
of a flower, Copenhagen

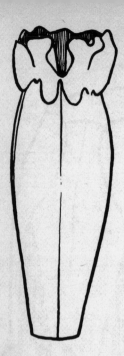

Emile Gallé

Copenhagen,
1900

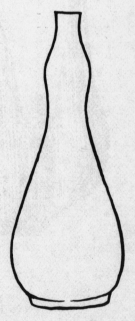

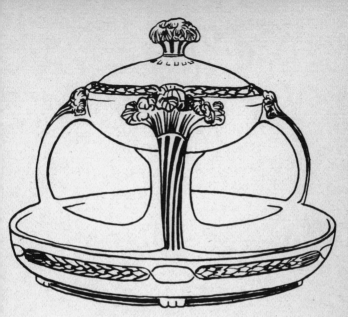

Dessert shell from the "Ceres" table service
by Theo Schmuz-Baudiss, Berlin 1912

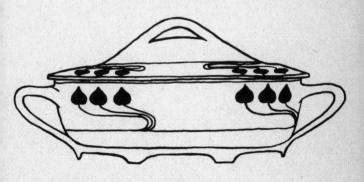

Tureen from a service by Philip Rosenthal

HISTORY OF
THE MANUFACTORIES

This chapter sketches the history of the most important manufactories. The choice of what to include depended mainly on
the aesthetic aspect of the development of porcelain.

Germany

Meissen (1710 to the present)

In 1709 Johann Friedrich Böttger arrived in Meissen to set up
a porcelain factory. On January 23, 1710, by royal decree a
porcelain manufactory was set up in Dresden, which in July
of the same year was shifted to the fortress of Albrechtsburg.
It employed twenty-five people. In the beginning it turned out
Böttger stoneware, the first great development in porcelain
creation. The stoneware forms were based on Chinese models
as well as influenced by work of contemporary silversmiths; it
was splendidly polished and had an incised or impressed decor.
In 1713, due to improvement in the hard glaze, porcelain became more important. The forms were at first designed by the
court goldsmith, Irminger.

Böttger died on March 13, 1719. From then until 1731 the
factory was totally under the influence of Johann Gregor
Höroldt who arrived from Vienna on April 2, 1720, along with
Samuel Stölzel. Copperplates were bought for patterns, but

Höroldt created his own designs, and determined the style of painting. Typical were the miniature paintings called "Höroldt Chinese." Blue underglazing became more and more popular. Part of this development was due to the production manager David Köhler, who worked with the Mehlhorns, father and son. Johann Gottfried Mehlhorn was one of the blue painters, then the great majority. Köhler's death in 1725 meant a resurgence for painting in blue, and by 1732 it predominated. In 1739 Johann David Kretschmar developed the famous *Zwiebelmuster* (onion pattern).

In 1731 Meissen had approximately forty painters, ten of whom specialized in blue painting. One of the best was Johann Georg Heintze. Johann Gottfried Klinger painted dusky flowers with shadows and insects; Adam Friedrich von Löwenfinck was a master of Indian flora. Many painters moved to other manufactories over the course of time, mostly to Vienna, Berlin, and Ansbach.

From 1727 the great mold maker at Meissen was Johann Gottlieb Kirchner. (He was discharged in 1728 but returned in 1730.) During his stay the ivory carver Johann Christian Ludwig Lücke was his assistant. In 1730 Kirchner was working on the life-size animals for the Japanese Palace. On June 22, 1731, Johann Joachim Kändler came to Meissen. He worked on the great commission for the Japanese Palace, along with Kirchner. That same year Kirchner left and Kändler finished the commission alone.

After that he concentrated on the creation of table services. His most famous work, the Swan Service, was made in 1737 for Count Brühl, who since 1733 had superintended the manufactory. Kändler was especially interested in small ceramics. His crinoline groups, comedy figures, tradesmen, and animals set the standard for European sculpture in porcelain. Besides Kändler, the other important modellers were Johann Friedrich Eberlein (1735–1749), Peter Reinicke (from 1743), and Friedrich Elias Meyer (1748–1761), a master of the Rococo, who later went to Berlin.

About 1740 the Rococo painting style came into the ascendent. The Chinese motifs disappeared, and around 1738 elegant scenes such as one finds in the paintings of Watteau began to

"Woman with Fan" by J.J. Kändler, Meissen, ca. 1740

Venice (Vezzi), ca. 1725

Sèvres: Tureen from
the Bird Service, 1759

Tureen from the Pearl Service by Auliczek with *grisaille* painting by Boehngen, Nymphenburg 1792–1795

Covered vase, so-called apothecary jar, Berlin, ca. 1775

Above: Meissen, ca. 1740, etched and black-glaze decor by Kanonikus von der Busch

Above: From the Hunt Service of Marquis Trivulzo, with Schwarzlot painting in gold, Vienna, Du Paquier, ca. 1740

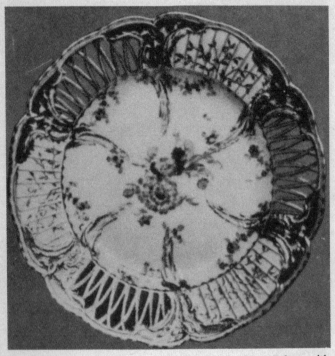

Above: Dessert tray from the Service for the New Palace with relief ornament and espalier, Berlin, 1765

Above: Kloster-Veilsdorf, plate with fruit painting

appear. In 1739 underglaze blue decor and *Zwiebelmuster* came together.

The manufactories suffered the effects of the second Silesian War (1744–1745), and especially the Seven Years War (1756–1763). Equipment and kilns were in ruins. Höroldt fled to Frankfort; Kändler stayed in Meissen. After the war these two great masters were no longer in demand. Höroldt retired in 1765 and Kändler worked with the new model master, Michel-Victor Acier (1764–1781). He was not successful, in part because neoclassicism was on the rise. Kändler died in 1775, having created approximately nine hundred models for Meissen.

From 1774 to 1813 the manufactory was under the directorship of Count Camillo Marcolini. The difficult economic situation caused by the war prevented him from becoming successful.

From 1814 to 1833 there was little technical innovation, probably because of the difficult economic situation at the time. Production conformed to the prevailing taste. Wedgwood ruled the field. In 1817 a chrome green underglaze was developed and the design of the vine-leaf pattern was inaugurated. In 1827 a gold glaze was invented by Heinrich Gottlieg Kühn.

The painter Ludwig Richter worked at Meissen from 1828 to 1835. In 1830 the royal manufactory became nationalized. In 1833 Kühn was appointed director. He held this post for thirty-seven years, during which time he encouraged and brought about many technical innovations. The kilns were improved and converted to coal, new porcelain pastes and colors were developed.

Under the leadership of his successor Raithel (1870–1894), Meissen researched new areas of chemical and technical improvement, as well as exploring established techniques. *Sang-de-boeuf* low-heat glazing was discovered as were *flambé* and crystalline glazes. The layered brush relief *(pâte-sur-pâte)* brought new life to designs as well. Besides blue and green, other underglazes were developed. Slowly, around the turn of the century Art Nouveau was adopted. In 1903 Henry van de Velde created a tea service for Meissen. Riemerschmid and Niemeyer created tableware. Paul Scheurich and Max Esser modelled figures.

1723—the first Höroldt mark: an imitation Chinese sign in underglaze blue.

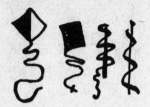

"Paper dragon" and "Mercury staff" for exported porcelain.

From April 7, 1723: Trademark for sugar bowl and small pot of a breakfast service.

K.P.M.: Royal Porcelain Manufactory; sometimes M.P.M., rarely K.P.F. 1725–1740, K.P.M. with swords. From 1740, only crossed swords. (Up to 1731, not every piece was signed.)

Until 1733 porcelain for the king was signed with the Augustus Rex mark. Friedrich August, 1733.

1725–1763

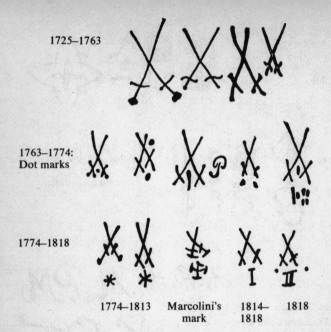

1763–1774:
Dot marks

1774–1818

1774–1813   Marcolini's   1814–   1818
                mark   1818

Royal service   KHC Royal *conditorei*
was marked   KHK Royal kitchen
to distinguish   KHKW Royal kitchen, Warsaw
different royal   KCPC Royal-princely Pillnitz *conditorei*
kitchens: CHK Princely kitchen
                     CPC Princely Pillnitz *conditorei*

Far right: Mark on
biscuit porcelain

1860–   1924–   since
1924   1934   1934

180

Far right: Jubilee mark

Two miscellaneous variants

Berlin (1751 to the present)

In 1751 the wool merchant Wilhelm Caspar Wegely obtained a privilege to found a porcelain factory in New Friedrichstrasse in Berlin. Despite the high quality of his product he was not successful, and financial difficulties finally forced him to resign. His business partner Reichard continued making porcelain, nevertheless.

In 1761 the merchant Johann Ernst Gotzkowsky purchased the factory and Reichard reorganized it on Leipzig Street, taking along all the old stock and models. The manager was Isaac Clauce; from Meissen came the famous modeler Friedrich Elias Meyer and the painters Karl Wilhelm Böhme (landscapes) and Johann Balthasar Borrmann; in 1763 the mosaic painter Karl Jakob Christian Klipfel arrived. The director was the Saxon councillor of commerce Johann Georg Greininger.

When Gotzkowsky fell into financial difficulties in 1763, Frederick the Great bought the factory for 225,000 talers, including all its incomplete stock and models.

Now began a period of great and continuous development, since the king took a personal interest in all aspects of the factory, doing everything to insure its success (holding a raffle, "Jewish porcelain"). He himself was its best customer, and his porcelain gifts to royalty (such as the famous centerpiece for

181

Catharine II of Russia) were at the same time excellent advertising. Berlin led in the design of services in the Rococo style. Meyer created a Service for the New Palace (1765), the Green Table Service and the Service for the Breslau State Palace (1767). In figure sculpture F. E. Meyer had no peer. Berlin floral painting was especially excellent.

Frederick's death in 1786 ended the liaison between the king and the manufactory.

Frederick Wilhelm II set up a royal porcelain manufactory commission. Despite rule by committee, during this period the manufactory continued to flourish. It created new glazes and colors, and when neoclassicism arose, it improved its pastes as well. Flat kilns replaced the round ones and the first steam boiler was set up in Prussia, ushering in the age of the boiler.

During the time of the Napoleonic wars the manufactory was compelled to work for the French. Only the skill of the director Rosenstiel saved the business. After the Peace of 1815 the plant recovered quickly. Many orders from Frederick Wilhelm III (the Military General Service) helped a lot. Biedermeier brought the painting of landscapes and scenes from daily life to a new level of achievement; leading artists such as Schinckel, Schadow, and Genelli gave of their best, after which began the general decline of nineteenth century porcelain creation. When the revival movement at the end of the century began, Berlin once again was the acme of German manufactories.

In 1878 a Commission of Artistic Reform was set up, comprising among others the artists Begas, Ewald, Jordan (director of the National Gallery), Lippmann (director of the Copper Engravers' Guild), Schöne (later General Director of the Museum), and the parliament member Lasker and Professor Virchow. In addition a chemotechnical institute was founded, which Hermann Seger headed. In 1881 the sculptor Sussmann-Hellborn became director, and in 1887 he was succeeded by the painter Professor Alexander Kips, by which time there were one hundred and fifty artist members.

With the nomination of Theo Schmuz-Baudiss from Munich Art Nouveau took over. The upshot of all this was that artists collaborated in the research work.

Famous mold makers were Adolf Amberg, Julius Feldmann,

and Paul Scheurich, and up to the first World War Ludwig Gies (under Nicola Moufang). In 1929 Moufang was replaced by Günther Freiherr von Pechmann. His was a much more managerial approach. He engaged artists such as Gerhard Marcks, Marguerite Friedländer-Wildenhain, and Trude Petri-Raben. In 1930 Berlin brought out the first undecorated white china, the Urbino Service of Trude Petri. Pechmann was succeeded by Werner Franke.

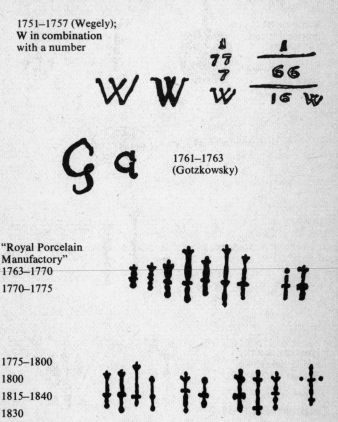

1751–1757 (Wegely);
W in combination
with a number

1761–1763
(Gotzkowsky)

"Royal Porcelain
Manufactory"
1763–1770

1770–1775

1775–1800
1800
1815–1840
1830

1837–1844

1844–1847

1847–1849

1849–1870

Scepter with
diagonal stroke,
1870–1945

Seger porcelain
since 1882

Jubilee mark,
1913

Since 1945
(Selb)

Painter's marks:
additional strokes
in blue 1803–1813;

in red 1817–1823;

eagle in red 1823–1832

Apple of Empire,
since 1832
in red, green, and blue

 KPM

 KPM

Since 1918: "Staatliche Porzellan-Manufaktur Berlin"

Fürstenberg, Braunschweig
(1753 to the present)

Because of mismanagement, Duke Karl I of Braunschweig got rid of his master of the hunt, Langen, who served as his arcanist, and got the director of the Höchst manufactory, Johann Kilian Benckgraff, for his Fürstenberg plant. In 1753 Benckgraff settled in Fürstenberg, bringing with him the painter Johann Zeschinger and the modeler and embosser Simon Feilner. Benckgraff died four weeks after his arrival, but at least by then Langer as arcanist was a thing of the past. Despite many technical difficulties, by the end of the year the plant began to prosper. Any further development hung fire during the Seven Years War, but by the end of 1769 things were improving once again under the leadership of the smelters Kaulitz and Kohl. Up through the eighties the manufactory flourished. Fürstenberg porcelain was being designed by accomplished painters. From 1762 on, among others, Johann Friedrich Weitsch ("Pasha") worked there as a painter. Some of the figure and relief sculptors were Simon Feilner (who in 1770 went to Mannheim and then to Frankenthal), Désoches (1769–1774), Carl Anton Luplau (until 1776), and Johann Christoph Rombrich (from 1758 on). Carl Göttlieb Schubert worked in Fürstenberg from 1775 to 1804.

Although figure sculpture was not the finest product of the manufactory, it can hold its own next to many original works. Désoches's figures had a Gallic charm; Luplau dealt with unusual themes, as in the engaging "Search for the Flea" and the "Old German Soldiers Playing Chess." But his best work were biscuit likenesses of contemporary personages.

From about 1790 standards began to slip. Louis Victor Gerverot (1795–1814) instituted a strict control of the plant. He was so unsuccessful in negotiations with Jerôme Bonaparte that from 1807 to 1813 the plant ceased production. From 1825 on there was a thirty-year period of able management under Stünkel. In 1859 the manufactory was leased, in 1876 sold outright, and in 1888 turned into a limited company.

Old marks

Eighteenth and
nineteenth centuries

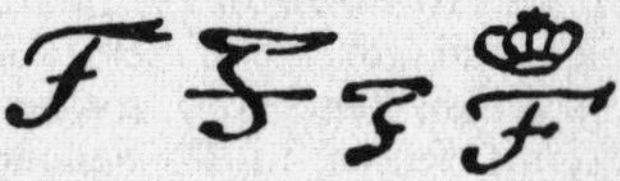

On modern china;

on reproductions
of old models;

the modern mark

The embossed signs on old
Feilner figures;

on biscuit busts
and reliefs

Höchst, Hessen (1750–1796)

Two merchants from Frankfort, Johann Christoph Göltz and Johann Felician Clarus joined up with the painter Adam

Friedrich von Löwenfinck on his leaving Meissen and founded a manufactory. In 1746 they obtained a fifty-year privilege from the Elector of Mainz, Johann Friedrich Karl von Ostein, to erect a porcelain factory. It only made faience. Löwenfinck had no knowledge about the manufacture of porcelain. He left Höchst in 1749.

Then in 1750, with the engagement of Johann Kilian Benckgraff, and Ringler's help on setting up some kilns based on Vienna design, they began to manufacture porcelain in earnest in Höchst. In 1753 Benckgraff went to Fürstenberg and took the painter Johannes Zeschinger and the modeler Simon Feilner with him.

Financial difficulties plagued the company until it went into bankruptcy in 1765 and reorganized as a limited company. The private claims of the shareholders were still too high. Finally, the majority stockholder, the Elector, Baron Emmerich von Breidbach, bought the manufactory. His successor as Elector, Baron Friedrich Karl Joseph von Erthal, in 1778 became the sole owner.

The strong point of the Höchst factory was its figure sculptures. From 1762 to 1767 Laurentius Russinger was the master modeler; he later went to Pfalz-Zweibrücken. The gifted modeler Johann Peter Melchior worked at Höchst from 1767 to 1799, after which he went first to Frankenthal and then to Nymphenburg.

In 1796 the enterprise ceased. Models and forms went to Daniel Ernst Müller's stoneware factory in Damm, near Aschaffenburg, and after 1840 were used for stoneware. They were passed on to the F.A. Mehlem stoneware factory in Bonn and in 1942 thirty of the forms were found in the porcelain factory of Phillip Dietrich in Passau.

marks until 1763

1750–1765

1762–1796

1765–1774

Johannes Zeschinger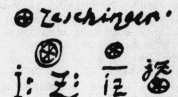

Adam Ludwig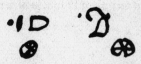

Philip Dannhofer

Simon Feilner

Frankenthal (1755–1800)

Paul Anton Hannong, a faience maker in Strasbourg, was not able to make any porcelain because the Vincennes state manufactory (Sèvres) held the monopoly. On May 26, 1755, he obtained a privilege to manufacture porcelain from the Elector Carl Theodor. In 1756 he began production in Frankenthal with the renowned model masters Johann Wilhelm Lanz (1756–1761) and Johann Friedrich Lück. When his oldest son Karl, who ran the factory, died in 1757, his younger brother Joseph Adam Hannong took over. In 1762, because of financial difficulties, he sold the place back to the sovereign and returned to Strasbourg, where he took over his recently-dead father's factory. Carl Theodor engaged the Mannheim sculptor Konrad Linck from Speyer (1732–1802), who went back to Mannheim in 1766, leaving behind many sketches and outlines. Until 1775 Karl Gottlieb Lück was model master. Adam Bergdoll, hitherto form maker in Höchst, became the new director of the royal porcelain manufactory, but he did not live up to expectations. So in 1770 Simon Feilner, model master in Fürstenberg, was taken on. Bergdoll was pensioned in 1775. Despite Feilner's strict reign—he improved the porcelain pastes and developed new colors—he could not overcome the economic situation. Adam Bauer was model master from 1777 to 1779, and from 1779 to 1793 Johann Peter Melchior came from Höchst to hold the position.

The figures from Frankenthal are of the first water. One of the most famous sculptors and creators of these remarkable figures was Konrad Linck.

He invested his bowls and china with high French standards. Frankenthal also employed the extraordinary figure painter Johann Bernhard Magnus from Osterspey and Winterstein.

With the rise of neoclassicism the Rococo style of ceramic was no longer profitable, and the inventory stock began to pile up.

In 1794 and 1795 Frankenthal let its French employees go, meanwhile leasing the factory to Peter van Recum of Grünstedt. After his departure the factory came more and

189

more under royal control.

In 1797 French troops occupied the left bank of the Rhine and the Frankenthal factory was nationalized.

Amid all these troubles, Simon Feilner died in 1798. Van Recum's successor, Johann Nepomuk van Recum, leaseholder of the factory, entered into a contract with the Prince of Leiningen, and returned to Grünstadt, taking along with him a great part of Frankenthal forms. A later owner of the factory gave the remaining forms to the Palatinate Textile Museum, later yet they were presented to the Palatinate Historical Museum in Speyer.

From 1900 to 1917, under the guidance of the Speyer Museum, the Frankenthal forms were lent to the Nymphenburg manufactory to recast new forms. These figures had as marks the Nymphenburg coat of arms with the crowned CT and the date of manufacture.

1755–1759

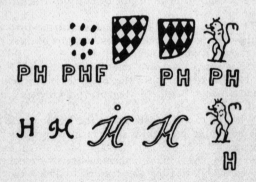

1759–1762

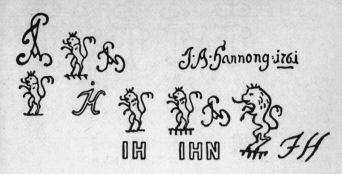

1762–1770

CT: Carl Theodor

1770–1789

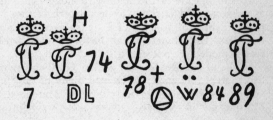

Ludwigsburg, Württemberg (1758–1824)

Duke Carl Eugen von Württemberg was an ostentatious ruler, and he felt porcelain was "essential to his pomp and dignity." In 1758, underwriting a private individual, he founded a manufactory, engaging Joseph Jakob Ringler as technical director. Ringler was one of the most influential porcelain makers of the century, although he is most known as an arcanist. Under his leadership the factory had its high point, from 1760 to 1767. He stands very high among figure modelers. Unfortunately, the factory's most artistically successful models are not signed.

In the age of Rococo the painter Gottlieb Friedrich Riedel had a great influence. He created many of the china designs, among others the service for the Marchesa Giovanelli-Martinengo in Venice. Others who were prominent are

Joseph Philip Dannhofer at Höchst, Johann Friedrich Steinkopf at Frankenthal, and Friedrich Kirchner at Bayreuth.

Ludwigsburg was the first German factory to convert to the neoclassic style. Duke Carl Eugen von Württemberg had sent Wilhelm Beyer to Rome to study, where Beyer became acquainted with Winckelmann's work. He returned in 1762, full of new ideas. Other famous modelers were Domenico Ferretti and Pierre François Lejeune.

In 1766 there were 154 people working in the manufactory. By 1770 the artistic level had sunk, however, and by the time of the death of Carl Eugen in 1793 quality had totally fallen off. King Wilhelm I closed the plant in 1824.

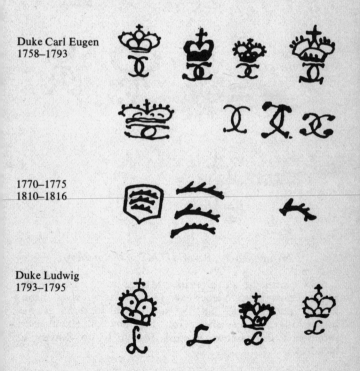

Duke Carl Eugen
1758–1793

1770–1775
1810–1816

Duke Ludwig
1793–1795

King Frederick
1806–1816

King Wilhelm
1816–1824

1948
"Former Royal
Manufactory
Ludwigsburg"

Nymphenburg, Bavaria (1747 to the present)

In 1747, with the aid of Prince Maximilian Joseph III, the potter Franz Ignaz Niedermayr founded a porcelain manufactory in Neudeck, but in vain. Then in 1753 it was successfully set up when Graf Sigmund of Haimhausen summoned the famous arcanist Joseph Jakob Ringler to Neudeck.

In 1754 Franz Anton Bustelli, one of the greatest ceramicists of the eighteenth century, came to Neudeck. He had the celebrated embosser Johann Georg Härtl model figures for him. In Bustelli's reign, Peter Anton Seefried (1756–1757) worked as modeler. The following painters were employed: Joseph Haslöder as blue painter, Franz Karl Rauffer, Andreas Philip Oettner, Andreas Ettner, and as chief painter Christoph Lindemann. Between 1760 and 1770 Josef Zächenberger was the head floral painter, and also taught his techniques to the others. In 1761 the Nymphenburg manufactory was transferred to a round chateau. Ambros Hermannsdorfer and the miniaturist Joseph Weiss together headed the classes in painting techniques.

In 1763 Bustelli died. He left behind an oeuvre of one hundred and fifty models. His last work was a bust of the Graf of Haimhausen. He was succeeded by Domenikus Auliczek, among whose best work is the outstanding Pearl Service (1792).

In 1767, the director Josef von Limprun had to let some of the three hundred employees go. In 1777 Prince Maximilian Joseph died, and the Bavarian title to the factory was passed onto the Elector Carl Theodor, who had lost his French appointment with the Frankenthal factory. Some artists went to Nymphenburg along with Peter Melchior. Some Frankenthal forms came thereby to the Nymphenburg manufactory. Later they were recast and they bore as a mark the Nymphenburg coat-of-arms in combination with the Frankenthal "CT." Auliczek retired in 1797 and Melchior was director until 1822. Among his creations was a simple Empire Service with a gold border.

Bustelli's models no longer expressed the spirit of the age and therefore the mayor gave Melchior instructions to destroy them.

The architect Friedrich Gärtner succeeded Melchior in Nymphenburg. He created the Onyx Service, which was totally in the spirit of classical antiquity with its gold meandering and ancient motifs in *grisaille* painting. Gärtner died in 1847; his successor was Eugen Napoleon Neureuther, who had very few connections to porcelain.

The artistic significance of the manufactory waned more

and more, to the point where Ludwig II had to get his porcelain from Meissen. Albert Bäuml saved the Nymphenburg enterprise from an ignoble end. He totally reorganized the works, returning to old, established forms and in 1890 he introduced the practical "ribbed" coffee and tea service we know today. Around 1900 they made Art Nouveau china (L. Levallois, later Adelbert Niemeyer). Painters at this time were Hermann Gradl and Rudolf and Ingrid Siek. Josef Wackerle created noteworthy figures (1910 "Woman with Muff," among others).

Albert Bäuml's sons run the factory today and besides the demand for new forms for figures and china, they are trying to bring back Bustelli's models as well. In 1927 Joseph Hillerbrand and Wolfgang von Wersin designed timely and handsomely formed china.

1754–1765, 1780–1790 (blind coat-of-arms mark)	
1800 1810 1850–1862 since 1862	
Modern mark	
From "Turkish Böcherl" ware	

1763–1767,
"Hexagram mark"

G z m ı Q 3

C.H.C. C.H.Z. C.H. Silberkaner
'77'

C. H. Conditorej
J7.
J 7 7 J

From modern copies
based on old
Frankenthal models
(date)

1948

1948

1948

Smaller German Manufactories

Ansbach-Bruckberg, Bavaria (1758–1860)

In a faience factory that had been producing since 1706, in
1758 the Margrave Alexander of the House of Hohenzollern
founded a factory for porcelain, probably with workers from
Meissen and Berlin. In 1762 the firm was transferred to his

hunting lodge in Bruckberg. The artistic director was the modeler Johann Friedrich Kändler, a cousin of Johann Joachim Kändler at Meissen. Other employees were: Gottlob Laut and Georg Ludwig Bartholomae as modelers, Kahl and Schreitmüller as blue painters, and Stenglein as landscape painter.

The miniaturist John Carl Gerlach worked at Ansbach from 1757 to 1759. Melchior Schöllhammer, who was his student from 1758 on, became assistant chemist and inspector in 1785 and in 1799 director of the manufactory.

In 1790 Ansbach fell to Prussia, in 1806 to Bavaria. Possibly because of competition with Nymphenburg the factory went downhill and in 1860 it was taken over by private individuals.

Because of excellent painting, the porcelain was handsomely executed, which above all accounts for Schöllhammer's success. The Ansbach patterns for china decor, although somewhat stiff, are very good.

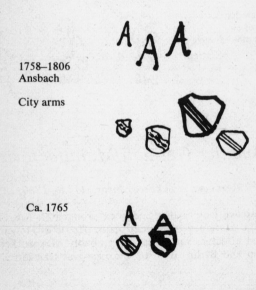

1758–1806
Ansbach

City arms

Ca. 1765

J.E.P.Leyln
Lündburg 18.Ap
1788

Kelsterbach, Hessen-Darmstadt (1758–1768)

The Landgrave Ludwig VIII of Hessen-Darmstadt in 1758 bestowed a privilege for a faience factory on the court hunter Wilhelm Cron and his brother-in-law, the faience maker Johann Christian Frede, who had worked as a lathe hand under Hannong. In 1759 Cron transferred his share over to his brother-in-law Casper Mayntz. In 1760 Mayntz acquired a suitable building for the manufactory in Kelsterbach and built a kiln. In 1761 Landgrave Ludwig VIII took over the firm and appointed Christian Daniel Busch as director. Busch had worked as a painter in Vienna and Meissen and in 1764 he went back to Meissen, taking over Höroldt's place.

An important modeler of the early days was Friedrich Carl Vogelmann; in 1767 a student of Bustelli, Peter Antonius Seefried, came from and in 1768 returned to Nymphenburg. Alongside Busch the painters from 1761 to 1764 were Georg Ignaz Hess and Franz Joseph Weber.

In 1765 the Cabinet Treasurer Eberhardt Dietrich Pfaff became director. In an effort to make the enterprise economically feasible he dismissed the master artists and instead took on mediocre craftsmen, who came and went frequently. Another economic step he took was to step up the production of faience, and he hired the grinder of the Offenbach faience factory, Philip Friedrich Lay, who stayed until 1766. With

Ludwig VIII's death the factory ceased operations and Pfaff retired.

The Höchst modeler Jakob Heinrich Höckel in 1802 tried to revive the plant but the project ran aground because of political circumstances.

Pfalz-Zewibrücken, Gutenbrunn
(1767–1775)

The arcanist and district medical officer Dr. Stahl and the modeler Laurentius Russinger set up a porcelain manufactory for Duke Christian IV in his Gutenbrunn chateau. Until 1768 the technical and artistic director was Russinger. The firm was closed in 1769 due to a flood in Zewibrücken. Russinger's successor was Jakob Heinrich Höckel from Höchst, whose brother oversaw the painters. Production ended in 1775 with the duke's death. The factory had concentrated almost exclusively on simply designed useful china with blue painting. Barely any figures were made.

With French and Saxon molds Wilhelm Heinrich von Nassau-Saarbrücken founded a manufactory in 1763 with the help of the arcanist Dominique Pellevé from Rouen. In the surrounding environs of Ottweiler they found quartz and kaolin and starting in 1764 they produced hard porcelain. For a short time in 1765 they employed Paul Louis Cyfflé, who didn't get along with Pellevé and was replaced with the modeler Tentz. Shortly thereafter Pellevé left Ottweiler.

After Prince Wilhelm Heinrich's death the factory was leased to the Frenchmen René François Jolly and Nicolas Leclerc. The painter from 1769 to 1770 was Karl Wohlfahrt. Ottweiler was the first factory to use bituminous coal in the form of coke to bake porcelain. In the 1780s production shifted over to the making of stoneware.

Ottweiler porcelain was of good quality. The decoration was especially noteworthy. Figurative works were rare; they concentrated on table and coffee services.

Fulda (1765–1780)

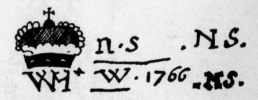

The ecclesiastical prince Henry VIII of Bibra founded at Fulda a "royal Fulda fine porcelain factory." His arcanist was Nikolaus Paul, a former worker of Wegely in Berlin.

Under the directorship of Abraham Ripp the factory turned out first-class small sculptures, reminiscent of those from Frankenthal and Meissen. Especially prominent are the refined colors and the exquisite decor of the figures. The china had sparse foregrounds. Some of the modelers were Wenzel Neu, Valentin Schaum, Johann Georg Schumann and Georg Ludwig Bartholome; some of the painters, Georg Friedrich and Johann Ignaz Hess.

In 1778 Adalbert von Harstall became eccleiastical prince and during his tenure, in 1789, the Fulda factory closed.

Kassel (1766–1788)

On May 6, 1766, the Landgrave Friedrich von Hessen founded a factory by the Weissenstein Gate. He enlisted the arcanist Nikolaus Paul from Fulda and in July of the same year they were able to start production. Many famous artists worked here, albeit for a short time—men such as the model master Johann Georg Pahland from Fürstenberg, the embosser Friedrich Künckler from Rudolstadt, the embosser Johann Joachim Hess from Fulda, the painters Georg

1764–1780, mark of the cross	
1780–1788, Heinrich's mark	
1788–1790, Adalbert's mark	

Schrimpf from Nymphenburg, Johann Zisler from Höchst, Johannes Uffelmann and Heinrich Eisenträger from Fürstenberg, and the blue painters Claudius Arend, Louis-Victor Gerverot and Jakob Dortu.

The last painted piece was made on June 24, 1788, because production had become unprofitable and the factory was closed. The huge inventory was sold cheaply.

Würzburg (1775–1780)

The ecclesiastical prince of Wurzburg, Franz Ludwig von Erthal, issued a privilege to his private chancellor and consistory advisor, Johann Kaspar Geyger, to operate until his death a small manufactory, where Geyger also worked as a painter. In 1776 the miniaturist H. Tünnich worked there a short time. The porcelain was of varied quality. Several surviving figures can be proved to have been made there.

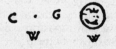

The rural inspector Arnold Friedrich Prahl founded a porcelain manufactory in 1758 in Utzemmingen. With the help of the Viennese arcanist Joseph Johann Ringler he was successful in getting production started. Prahl died in 1758 and his widow moved the business to Ellwangen. There they produced porcelain for a year, but the neighboring Bux faience factory in Schrezheim caused constant problems and finally the factory ceased operations.

The arcanist Ringler worked with the painters Johann Andreas Bechdorff, Jörg Adam Keyb, the father-and-son Hess team, and the embosser Josef Nees, who later went to Ludwigsburg and then Zürich.

They manufactured china, vari- and blue-painted courtly and general figures.

Thüringia

In contrast to most German porcelain makers, the majority of the Thüringian firms were privately owned, and built as commercial enterprises depending on private consumption. They received no subsidies and therefore above all were affected by the financial means of the people who patronized them. The famous artists of the great factories were not Thüringian woodsmen, after all, though in their charm and in their natural vigor the products have a down-to-earth appeal. The figures especially have a rustic charm about them.

Independently, Georg Heinrich Macheleid was successful in inventing a porcelain paste. In 1760 Prince Johann Friedrich of Schwarzburg-Rudolstadt gave him the privilege of founding a porcelain factory. The factory abandoned by von Sitzendorf in Volkstedt in 1762 filled the bill. The prince belonged to the Volkstedt nobility as well, and on his death in 1767 the factory was leased to Christian Nonne, who led it for thirty-three years. Macheleid retired with a life annuity. In 1797 the factory was bought by Prince Ernst Constantin of Hessen-Philipsthal, who, two years later, sold it to the merchants Wilhelm Heinrich Immanuel Greiner and Carl

Macheleid

1760–1799

1787
The modified marks
after the
Meissen injunction

Modern marks
("Oldest Volkstedt
Porcelain Factory")

Gottfried Holzapfel. The manager of the firm of Greiner
and Holzapfel was Greiner's son Anton, who took over the
factory on his father's death in 1817 and ran it until 1826.
After that the business changed hands many times.

In the beginning (1765) the painters were Johann Andreas
Greiner and Triebner, and the embosser was Künckler from
Fürstenberg. The chief artist for eight years was the court
painter, Franz Kotta.

The china was often most originally designed and sculpted.
Mostly the forms were based on Meissen, and the figures
were painted with distinction.

Kloster-Veilsdorf (since 1760)

Prince Friedrich Wilhelm Eugen of Hildburghausen founded
a manufactory in 1760 with the help of the arcanist Johann
Hermann Meyer, who shortly thereafter died. The kilns were
built to the specifications of Nikolaus Paul, but he didn't
work at the factory. His son, however, worked there from
1763 to 1771.

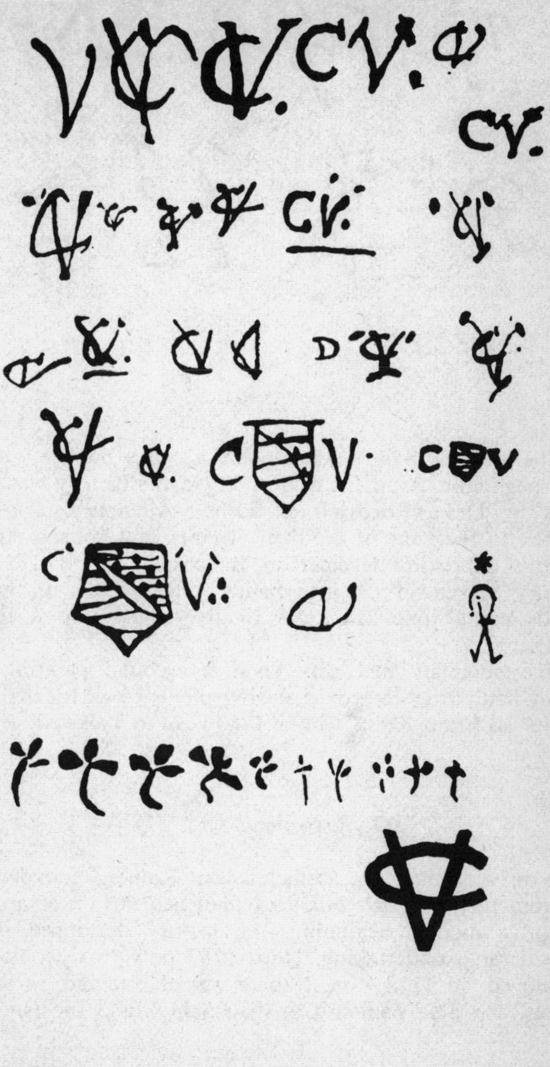

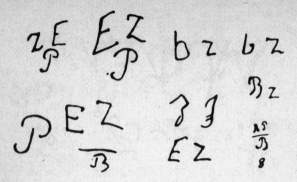

The prince tried to make a go of the place but the outcome was negligible. After his death in 1795 the factory was taken over by Duke Friedrich of Sachsen-Altenburg, who then sold it to the sons of Gotthelf Greiner in Limbach and the firm of Christian Greiner in Rauenstein. Until 1822 the factory stayed in Greiner hands, after which it changed hands many times and was finally turned into a limited company.

The porcelain had very good foreground painting. The figure sculptures improved during the 1770s. Modeler for a while was Franz Kotta, who in 1783 went to Volkstedt.

Gotha (from about 1757)

The privy councillor Wilhelm von Rotberg founded this manufactory in 1757. Nikolaus Paul helped him as arcanist. From a modest beginning, the factory developed into a considerable undertaking. Until 1767 only two people were employed. In 1772 Von Rotberg was able to hire three able artists, the blue painter Christian Schulz and the landscape

1757–1783

1783–1805

Since 1805

1830
"Henneberg"

209

and historical painters Johann Georg Gabel and Johann Adam Brehm, who worked as modelers. They determined the artistic policy and leased the factory for ten years until 1788. The firm of Schulz and Co. proved successful.

On Von Rotberg's death in 1795, his widow sold the factory to the hereditary prince, August von Gotha, and he put in his valet, Egidius Henneberg, as overseer and director. In 1804 Henneberg leased the factory and by 1813 he owned it. He died in 1834. He was succeeded by his son, who ran the firm till 1860; it was run by his godson August Henneberg until 1881.

Of all the Thuringian manufactories Gotha produced the best china. Small services with fine painted decors and, later, silhouette cups and excellent vases, were its specialties. Figure ceramics were restricted to biscuit.

Wallendorf (from 1764)

Johann Wolfgang Hamann, acquainted with mining and metallurgical engineering, got together with the potter Johann Georg Dümmler, the glazier Gotthelf Greiner, and his brother-in-law Gottfried Greiner and founded a porcelain manufactory in Limbach. The Greiners had developed a good paste and a good enamel glaze. The concession from Duke Anton Ulrich von Meiningen wasn't auspicious because of a meager timber supply. Finally Hamann bought the Wallendorf manor. With a privilege from Duke Franz Josias von Koburg-Saalfeld, it was there in 1764 that the factory was set up. By the 1790s the labor force numbered more than fifty. In 1771 Gotthelf Greiner went to Limbach and set up his own factory. In 1776 Hamann leased the factory to his son Ferdinand Friedrich, who bought it outright in 1782. From his death in 1786 on, his widow ran it until their son took it over in 1811.

In 1794 Johann Heinrich Hutschenreuther founded a workshop in which he, along with four other painters painted Wallendorf porcelain. After many changes of ownership the manufactory was incorporated in 1897.

Besides excellent practical china the factory produced fine wares. Dark glazes worked with recessed vari-colored paintings were a Wallendorf specialty. The figures of the early years were especially lively in their execution.

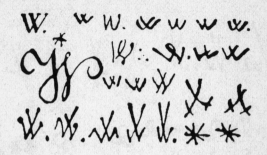

Limbach (1772)

Gotthelf Greiner succeeded in setting up his own factory. The concession for a porcelain factory in Limbach was not afforded free supplies, so he developed a partnership with Wolfgang Hamann and his brother-in-law Gottfried in Wallendorf. In 1771 he managed to renew the concession granted by the royal chambers in Meiningen and in 1772 he began production, which proved successful. In 1792 his five sons took over the factory. He died in 1797. His sons ran the firm under the name Gotthelf Greiner's Sons.

Above all, the china here was renowned for its use of fine pastes. The blue painting (stalk design) was especially refined. On an even higher rung stand the figures. Noteworthy are the *putti* figures representing the seasons of the year.

Many of the figures are not totally successful since the painting is somewhat flawed. Nevertheless the costume figures are quite charming.

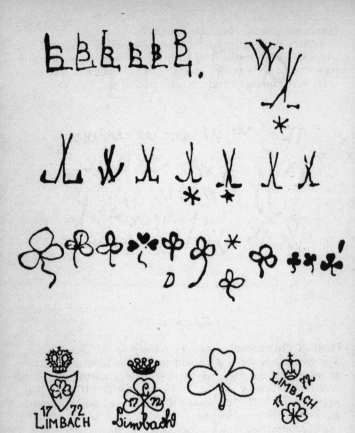

Limbach 1772—first marks under Greiner

Gera (1779)

The state pipe manufacturer, Johann Gottlob Ehwaldt, hoped that in partnership with the faience maker Johann Gottlieb Gottbrecht he could make a suitable ground porcelain and

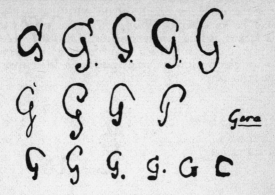

set up a business. For this the Landgrave Heinrich XX of Reuss gave him a building, but the porcelain manufactory was not successful. In 1780 he sold the business to the Greiner brothers, who owned the factory at Volkstedt. There were constant disputes over the factory. In 1800 Georg Wilhelm Greiner's widow worked out an arrangement whereby she brought another partner into the business. Until 1815 Gustav Heinrich Leer was joint owner and it was he who improved the state of affairs.

The forms of the china were in the neoclassic style. They produced chiefly presentation cups. Gera figures are rare.

Ilmenau (from 1777)

In 1777 Christian Zacharias Gräbner of Grossbreitenbach got a concession from Duke Carl August von Weimar to erect a porcelain factory. Gräbner incurred many debts, and so in 1782 the factory came under royal administration.

It was leased from 1786 to 1792 to Gotthelf Greiner. His successor was Christian Nonne, who had headed the Volkstedt factory. Around 1800 under Nonne the firm produced portrait reliefs and white biscuit medallion reliefs on a pale blue ground in imitation of Wedgwood's blue jasper ware. By 1808 Nonne and his son-in-law Ernst Karl Rösch were joint owners of the factory. When Nonne died in 1813 Rösch ran the plant alone, with few happy results. In 1871 it became a limited company.

Grossbreitenbach,
Thuringia

Ilmenau, Thuringia
1788–1792

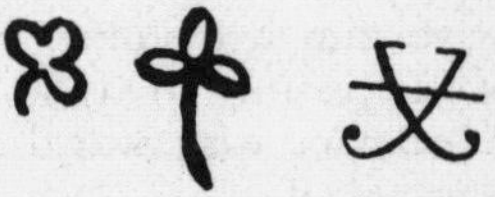

1792–1808

1808

N&R

Hohenberg (Bavaria)

Founded in 1814
by Carl Magnus
Hutschenreuther

In the 19th century, more and more new factories were founded which today are huge establishments, many privately owned and managed. They had to be economically profitable, besides having to overcome all the various crises—political, social, etc.—of the 19th century. The greatest of these, Hutschenreuther and Rosenthal, exerted themselves to keep abreast of the times, particularly at the end of the century with the rise of Art Nouveau.

215

Arzberg (Bavaria)

1839,
Carl Magnus
Hutschenreuther

1881,
Carl Schumann

Selb (Bavaria)

1856,
Lorenz
Hutschenreuther

1866,
Jakob Zeidler

JZ & Co.

1867,
Philip
Rosenthal

1884,
Krautheim and
Adelberg

1896,
Heinrich & Co.

Kronach (Bavaria)
1897,
Philip Rosenthal & Co.

Unterweissbach
(Thuringia)
Mann and Porzelius,
Schwarzburg workshop.

Before World War I the following worked at this manufactory:
Ernst Barlach, Paul Scheurich, later, Ludwig Gies.

AUSTRIA

Vienna (1717–1864)
The Time of du Paquier 1717–1744
("Vienna Before the Mark")

Claudius Innocentius du Paquier founded a porcelain manufactory in Rossau in Vienna with a concession from the Trier war council. He had studied the Entrecolles documents from China and hoped that, with the help of the Meissen gilder Christoph Conrad Hunger, he could fire porcelain that year, but Böttger beat him to it by designing a kiln and in 1718 the Meissen arcanist Samuel Stölzel came to Vienna. Because of the poor economic state of the enterprise, Stölzel went back to Meissen, taking the painter Gregor Höroldt with him. The same year, Hunger went to Venice. Du Paquier moved his factory to Porzellangasse (Porcelain Alley) and took on more help.

One of Hunger's rarer creations was an expensive goblet for the king, with fine gold relief embedded with small rubies and turquoises.

Characteristic of production at this time—until around 1730—was chinoiserie (pieces invested with the Kaiser's mark, in Chinese style) and the influence of the Viennese Baroque (foliage work and lace filigree). Many were painted in Schwarzlot and partially decorated in gold. The Viennese manufactory first brought out strawflower decoration, then Indian flowers and later German flowers.

Du Paquier was senior painter among a group of fine workers and distinguished painters (Bottengruber from Breslau, Helchis from Vienna, Carl Wendelin Anreiter von Zirnfeld, Anton Franz Josef Schulz) and produced the best colors of the time on Viennese porcelain. Among other painters one should mention Joseph Philip Dannhöfer, who went to Höchst via Bayreuth.

The porcelain of the du Paquier period has few relations to Meissen. The forms were individually developed. Special mention should be made of the slim chocolate cup with baroque pipe ornamentation on the underside, with or without handles, and with a deep saucer (*trembleuse*), and china with figure sculptures.

In spite of successful production, du Paquier was in constant financial difficulty which compelled him finally to sell the manufactory, now employing twenty people, to Maria Theresa. He was pensioned in 1751 and died the same year.

The State Period (1744–1784)

During this time there occurred the transition from Rococo to Neoclassicism, when Vienna created works based on Sèvres patterns.

It was in 1744 that Vienna porcelain was marked with the shield mark. Until 1749 it was in red or blue underglaze, with a dull stamp engraved or embossed. From then until 1827 the shield mark was in underglaze blue.

In 1749 they were able to greatly improve the paste. From 1750 to 1780 pieces for the palace were marked with a special shield mark in underglaze blue.

On low-quality goods either a red or green A was placed over the blue mark or conspicuously incised over it. From 1783 on the date was impressed next to the mark, for example 85 for 1785 or 806 for 1806. Stamped letters are embossed into the piece, the numbers marked in with paint. From 1827 until 1850 the shield mark appeared more and more often.

The new era as a state manufactory was characterized by a strict organization. Old stock on hand was disposed of in lots, and the firm expanded. During the two Silesian wars many artists came to Vienna from Meissen. From 1745 on, the head painter and director was Anton Anreiter von Zirnfeld and the overpainter was Johann Sigismund Fischer; also Christian Daniel Busch and Samuel Hitzig from Meissen. In 1746 the floral painter Johann Gottfried Klinger went to Meissen as a color consultant. Originally from Meissen, the floral painter Johann Daffinger left Vienna and went to Zürich in 1770. Famous modelers were Josef Niedermayer (1747–1784), who created national and later neo classic figures; Leopold Dannhauser, who worked in Neoclassic style according to Sèvres patterns; Anton Grassi (1755–1807) and Filippo Taglioni.

In 1784, due to economic difficulties, the manufactory was put up for sale. Not much interest was aroused except for the noble Linz textile manufacturer Konrad von Sorgenthal (Sörgel) who was in his element at the rise of Neoclassicism, the time of the injection of new blood into industry. His molds were created by Anton Grassi, then later by Niedermayer, who worked mainly in biscuit porcelain. The simple china forms were decorated with gold relief by the painters Georg Perl (1771–1807) and Joseph Leithner, using ancient models and to some extent newly created ground colors.

Although Sorgenthal died in 1805, the factory continued on in the same mode till around 1820. The Vienna manufactory was subject to the general decline of the time. In 1864 it was liquidated. Many took advantage of this occasion to buy up undecorated porcelain in volume and later had it painted in other factories.

Some imitations of "Old Vienna Ware" are by Franz Dörfl (since 1880) or Josef Vater (since 1850).

The present Vienna manufactory in Augarten was founded in 1922.

du Paquier,
1720–1730

State period
1744–1784

1744–1749

1749–1780

1750–1780

Sorgenthal Period
1784–1864

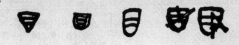

1820–1827
1827–1850
1850–1864
Foreclosure

Bohemia

Schlaggenwald (1793)

Franz Anton Haberditzel was the founder of the Bohemian porcelain industry. In 1789 he had erected a porcelain factory with the porcelain dealer Jakob Just of Thuringia in Rabensgrün near Schlaggenwald, but it stood idle until 1793.

Graf von Kaunitz, lord of Rabensgrün, on June 18, 1791, bestowed on the mayor Johann Georg Paulus and the arcanist Johann Georg Reumann of Hildburghausen (Thuringia) a grant for the founding of a porcelain factory on his property.

The high point of the undertaking came in the period from 1820 to 1840, when Haas and Lippert were the owners.

From 1876 the factory was called Haas and Czjzek, from 1904 Sommer and Matschak.

FIG 268

Lippert and Haas

Haas and Czjzek

Sommer and Matschak

Elbogen
1815, Rudolf Eugen Haidinger
(along with Epiag
from 1923)

Heinrich Kretschmann

1902,
Adolf Persch

FRANCE

St. Cloud, Seine-et-Oise (1678–1766)

Pierre Chicaneau founded this manufactory in 1678 and turned out a very good soft paste porcelain. On his death his widow took over, then remarried. Her new husband, Henri Charles Trou, ran the factory under letters patent from the Duke d'Orleans (Louis XIV's brother).

The *pâte tendre* (frit porcelain) of St. Cloud has an exterior resemblance to *blanc de Chine*. The glaze is fine and with a silky luster.

The decoration and the forms in the early period are closely related to Rouen faience. Louis Poterat created in Rouen around 1763 a soft paste porcelain like faience, decorated predominantly in blue under the glaze, not relying at all on Chinese motifs.

Sunburst

After 1722 (Henry Charles Trou)

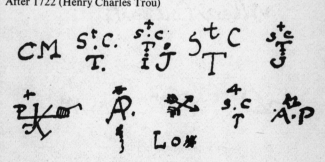

In St. Cloud, besides imitating Japanese and Chinese models, they learned how to add more colors to the glazes. By 1740 the forms show a Meissen influence and display more knowledge of the working of silver.

Figures were quite rare since the pastes were not suitable.

Chantilly, Oise (1725–1800)

The manufactory was founded in 1725 by Louis Henri de Bourbon, Prince de Condé, and run by Ciquaire Cirou until 1751. Then the directorship changed greatly. In 1792 the Englishman Christopher Potter, an expert in Paris hard paste porcelain, took it over. He had to give it up in 1800 because of financial difficulties.

New establishment, 1803

The factory's best hour was under Cirou, when a soft, milky tin-ash glaze (as in faience) was used. Forms and patterns were close to Japanese models, above all the work of Kakiemon. A favorite motif was the partridge in blue or red. Around the middle of the 18th century a stronger influence from Vincennes was felt, where the Rocaille style of the Louis XV period was in the ascendent.

In painting there often appeared the Meissen "German flowers" and the Boucher *putti* in purple *camaïeu* (tone on tone). Vincennes had the monopoly on color painting. The high-temperature palette with fine gold patterns also had its model at Vincennes-Sevres.

A second manufactory was founded at Chantilly in 1803 by Pigory. Here they made hard porcelain. The most important are the biscuit figures based on the works of Pradier. In 1845 Michel-Isaak Aaron took over the business.

Mennecy-Villeroy, Seine-et-Oise (1734–1806)

In 1734 François Barbin founded a faience factory in Paris, which he moved to Mennecy in 1748. Protected by the Duke of Villeroy, Louis-François de Neufville, father and son Barbin produced conventional soft paste porcelain until 1765, when they brought into the business Joseph Jullien and S. Jacques, who already were running a factory at Sceaux (1763–1794), and the two establishments were merged. In 1733 they had bought Sceaux as well as a factory that was located on the Bourg-la-Reine in Paris, which lasted until 1806.

Early Mennecy porcelain readily imitated St. Cloud and Chantilly wares, as well as Chinese models, and later Sèvres also. Characteristic of Mennecy was a brilliant shiny milk-white glaze.

It was quite difficult to make figures in *pâte tendre*. Nevertheless some of their figures are of high quality, especially some sensitively painted children's groups in the Boucher style. Also they made some good figures in biscuit.

Mennecy-Villeroy

DV: de Villeroy;
incised or painted
in red or blue

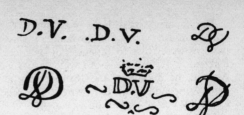

Sceaux

Bourg de la Reine

The most famous French manufactory was set up in 1738 under the patronage of the Marquis Orry de Fulvy (brother of Louis XV's finance minister) to create Saxon-style porcelain. He set up workers from Chantilly in his unoccupied Vincennes chateau and for three years they worked in vain to create a good paste. Finally the Dubois brothers and François Gravant succeeded in creating a good soft paste in 1745. They set up a firm and the king granted them a subsidy as partners in the undertaking.

The factory was headed by Jean Hellot, a chemist from the Parisian Academy. The illustrious artistic team was comprised of the master goldsmith Duplessis, the enamel expert Mathieu, and the overglazer Bachelier.

In 1753 the factory was allowed to call itself the "royal manufactory of French porcelain." It alone had the monopoly on varicolored wares. It was, needless to say, hard going for other manufactories, which could only use monochromatic decoration. The LL was the factory mark. The king had a thirty-three percent share in the profits.

In 1756 the factory was moved to Sèvres. Because of constant and bitter disagreements among the stockholders, in 1759 the king took the factory under his own management.

Sèvres porcelain was simply designed, with elegant forms (which required soft materials), painted in wonderful colors, and was fired under low temperatures. The very early Vincennes porcelain for the most part is unpainted. The famous colored backgrounds were developed by Hellot. Famous are his *bleu de roi*, the cloudy *gros bleu* and *bleu mourant*, his *Turkis* and his most beautiful *rose pompadour*, which he was not able to achieve in hard porcelain. Later for hard porcelain Sèvres created darker background colors. Characteristic of Sèvres were the colorful floral and fruit painting on recessed panels. Many background colors were finely gilded, such as the marvelous *oeil-de-perdrix* (partridge eye); diaper arrangement in circularly arranged points and stars.

In contrast to other manufactories, Sèvres allowed its

painters to sign their works, so no one worked there anonymously.

In 1752 Bachelier introduced biscuit porcelain, which influenced all of European Neoclassic sculpture. Etienne-Maurice Falconet was the preeminent Sèvres sculptor in this style. The painter François Boucher supplied patterns, although he didn't work at the manufactory. A very popular and extremely profitable specialty of the middle of the eighteenth century was flowers in porcelain, pots originally and richly decorated as if they were bejeweled, and special pieces with gilt-bronze handles, and other fashionable articles. Madame de Pompadour kept all of hers in a greenhouse!

In 1772 Sèvres began to make hard porcelain, which had been developed in 1768 by a Limoges kaolin worker. In 1777 they started making biscuit in hard porcelain. Many biscuit figures were based on already famous works in marble. The model masters in the 1770s were Bachelier, Leclerc, and Louis-Simon Boizot; the chief painter was Genest.

The jewel porcelain (*porcelain à émaux*), with soft gold-plate and colored molten enamel on a blue or Turkish-colored ground, was more of a technical achievement than an artistic one.

In 1780 Sèvres's monopoly on varicolored painting was broken.

Despite troubles during the revolution, the manufactory continued producing. Alexander Brogniart was director from 1780 to 1847. It was under his leadership that in 1800 hard porcelain started being produced. During the First Empire, the time of Napoleon, Sèvres set the standard in Europe. In 1804 it acquired the title of royal porcelain manufactory. Brogniart's successor, Ebelmann, sought in vain to continue making soft porcelain, at which Sèvres previously had excelled. Until 1870, that is, when a new paste was created. On Ebelmann's death, Regnault became director (1852–1871); the artistic director was Dieterle, then Nicolle. In 1876 the factory was run by Carrière-Belleuse, Charles Lauth, and Georges Vogt. From 1887 to 1891, under Théodore Deck, Sèvres experienced a brief technical resurgence. Among other artistic directors were Emil Baumgart and Alexandre Sandier.

In 1909 Emile Bourgeois took over the plant and in 1920 Lechevallier-Chévignard. Sculptors at various times were A. Rodin and A. Léonard; painters Taxile Doat, Solon, and H. Lasserre.

Marks: 1738–1744 in Vincennes, two touching, winding *L*'s; between 1745 and 1752 a point was added. Since 1753, the year's characters are shown with the lozenge-shaped *L*'s. Eventually the name appeared with the doubled letters. From 1769 to 1793 on hard porcelain the kingly crown was added to the letters. The marks appear mostly in bright blue. During the Revolution many marks appeared rather indistinguishably: *RF* in Italic cursive script intwined in each other, or the monogram with the name *Sèvres.* Between 1800 and 1802, *Sèvres* alone in gold script. Under Napoleon's consulship (1803–1804), *M.N. de Sèvres;* under the First Empire (1804–1809), *M. Imp. le de Sèvres;* 1810 to 1814, the crowned eagle on the fasces under which *Manufacture Imperiale Sèvres* was stamped in red. Toward the end of the eighteenth century, many small private manufactories sprang up, making hard porcelain. They were mostly under some kind of princely protection, but they had few similarities to the great government manufactory.

Before 1753

Mark with crown and letters

R = 1770
until
PP = 1793

First Republic
1793–1804

Consulat
1803–1804

First Empire
1804–1814

Right:
1810–1814

Louis XVIII
1814–1824

Charles X
1824–1830

Louis Philippe
1830–1848

Wedgwood pot from the famous colored jasper ware (stoneware) with white relief, end of 18th century

Coffee service with mythological painting, Nymphenburg, ca. 1810

Above: "Meleager and Atalanta," Konrad Linck, Frankenthal,
ca. 1770

Above: Princesses Louise and Friederike, biscuit porcelain, Gottfried Schadow, Berlin, 1796

Vase by Arnold Krog, underglaze blue painting based on Japanese woodcut, "The Wave" by Hokusai; Copenhagen, 1888

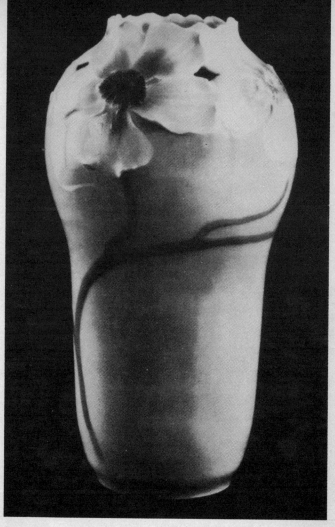

Art Nouveau vase with narcissus border,
Rörstrand, Sweden, ca. 1900

French Art Nouveau vase, ca. 1900

Japanese man as centerpiece for wedding of the German crown prince; Adolf Amberg, 1905

Teapot with gold ornamentation, designed by Henry van de Velde, Meissen, 1903

Second Republic,
1848–1852

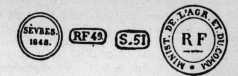

Second Empire,
1852–1870

Soft porcelain

Third Republic,
since 1871

On porcelain
Théodore Deck
developed

On biscuit porcelain,
1860–1899

SEVRES

1928–1940

Since 1941

SÈVRES
MANUFACTURE
NATIONALE
FRANCE

Among them, in 1769 Peter Hannong founded a factory in the Faubourg St. Lazare that was under the protection of Philippe, Count d'Artois; the manufactory of the duc d'Angoulème was founded by Guerhard and Dihl in 1780 in the rue de Bondy, actively in competition with Sèvres; and the manufactory "*dites à la Reine*" founded by André-Marie Leboeuf and patronized by Marie Antoinette.

There was an important small faience manufactory founded in Niderviller (Lothringia) in 1754 by Baron Jean-Louis de Beyerle. From 1770 to 1793 it was run by Count de Custine, from 1793 to 1827 by Claude-François Lanfrey. Charles-Gabriel Sauvage did the excellent figures in biscuit and painting as well from 1759 to 1808. He was succeeded by his son Lemire. In 1827 M.L.G. Dryander took over the plant.

1754–1770
De Beyerle

1770–1793
Count de Custine,
CC and CN

Since 1768, when a kaolin deposit was discovered in St. Yrieix near Limoges, there have been many small manufactories, not only in Paris, but right up to the present in Limoges as well.

In 1771 the Grellet brothers founded a factory which until 1784 stood under the protection of the Count d'Artois. Then the king took over the business and from then on white porcelain was painted in Sèvres.

Especially important as to the development of Art Nouveau was the arrival in 1842 of David Haviland from England to found a factory. In the 1860s he rejected the historically oriented painting of the time. He actually made very few new forms, but his individual and special kind of decoration pointed the way for many artists to the new style.

1827

1793–1827
"Lemire père"
(Charles-Gabriel
Sauvage)

Mark CD: Count
d'Artois

241

SWITZERLAND

Zürich (1763–1790)

In Schoren near Bendlikon, close to the Lake of Zürich, in 1763 a limited company was set up, encouraged by the scientific community to analyze the minerals and earth in the canton of Zürich. Among the stockholders were members of the Heidegger family, to which the writer and the pastoral painter Salomon Gessner belonged. The technical and artistic director was the faience maker Adam Spengler; the business duties were undertaken by Martin Usteri.

Despite encouraging results the factory fell into economic difficulties. In 1791 the business was sold. The high point of its history was from 1763 to 1790, when it employed the painters Gessner, Heinrich Füssli, and, above all, Johann Daffinger. Daffinger created the famous Kloster Hermit Service. Lifelike, the figures were painted by Valentin Sonnenschein, Josef Nees, and Spengler's son, who eventually went to Derby.

$$Z \quad \underset{\bullet\bullet}{Z} \quad \neq 3$$

Nyon (1781–1813)

Ferdinand Müller and his son-in-law Jakob Dortu, who was somewhat knowledgeable about porcelain, founded a factory on Lake Geneva, chiefly to produce useful chinaware. Dortu, who came from a family that had emigrated from France, had learned blue and varicolor painting in Berlin and had even set up his own factory (1777–1778) where he made hard porcelain in Marieberg in Sweden. At Nyon he served as technical and artistic director. The firm turned out good works handsomely painted, especially in floral painting. Figures were rarely made.

In 1809 the manufactory was made into a limited company. It stopped producing in 1813.

Dortu and Cie.,
19th century

"Fine pottery
Bonnard and Gonin",
19th century

D C

DORTU & Cie

"Pfluger frère and Co.",
19th century

ENGLAND

Chelsea, West London (1743–1784)

The founders of the manufactory were two Frenchmen, the goldsmith Charles Gouyn and the silversmith Nicholas Sprimont. In 1749, six years after it was founded, Gouyn left the partnership.

We can distinguish the marks of four periods at Chelsea: The Triangle Period (1745–1749), the Relief Anchor Period (1750–1753), the Red Anchor Period (1753–1756) and the Gold Anchor Period (1758–1769). The manufactory was shut down from 1756 to 1758, and in 1770 it was merged by William Duesbury with his Derby factory. From then until 1784 was the Chelsea-Derby Period.

In the Triangle Period silver pots were made and painted with flowers along Meissen lines. Figures were quite rare. The Anchor Relief Period conformed to Chinese patterns of *blanc de Chine* and Arita porcelain, later to Meissen models.

The Red Anchor Period is the high point of the art of porcelain in England. The famous Chelsea Toys come from this and the Gold Anchor Period. Meissen was the standard, but during the Gold Anchor Period, above all Sèvres was copied. The colors *gros bleu* and *rose Pompadour* were called, in England, Mazarin blue and claret.

All Anchor Period ware got its artistic inspiration from Sprimont. Because of ill health he was compelled to offer the factory up for sale in 1763. He died in 1771. In 1770 James Cox who had purchased it sold it to William Duesbury, who merged it with his Derby factory. The so-called Chelsea-Derby Period was typical of the age of Neoclassicism.

Bow, East London (1744–1778)

The merchant Edward Heylyn and the coppersmith Thomas Frye established a glassworks in Bow. In 1744 they acquired letters patent to manufacture porcelain. However, with a new patent for bone china and the financial help of the merchants Weatherby and Crowther, they were able to set up a porcelain manufactory and make it productive by 1749. The factory is still called "New Canton." It was oriented toward the tastes and fancies for Japanese and Chinese models, especially *blanc de Chine* and Chinese blue-and-white porcelain and *famille rose* decoration. At this time the Irish engraver John Brooks invented his transfer process, and in 1755 Bow took on the engraver Robert Hancock, who was the most important master of this technique. He went to Worcester in 1757.

With copperplate engraving they were able to incise fireproof colors. They would apply fine paper bearing the patterns and then withdraw it from the porcelain, having transferred the pattern thereby. For stoneware especially this process was of the greatest importance. Bow also brought out simply modeled, very attractive figures.

Frye took over the management in 1759 and died in 1763; Weatherby had died in 1762. In 1763 Crowther went into bankruptcy and in 1776 Duesbury took over the factory. He closed the factory in 1778 and moved the models to Derby.

Pfeile, before 1750

Embossed marks,
1750–1760

"New Canton",
1750–1770

Derby, Derbyshire (1756 to the present)

In 1745 Thomas Briand and James Marchand set up a manufactory, which operated only a short while. In 1756 the **enamel painter William Duesbury**, with the help of André Planché and the banker John Heath, founded a manufactory whose product he offered as "Derby or the second Dresden." He wanted the public to confuse his ware with Meissen.

The figures had no marks, except for two to four scratches derived from the firing supports. In 1769 John Bacon modeled fine figures.

Early on, they were making biscuit figures based on Sèvres models. From about 1770 to 1774, the mold makers Pierre Stephan and Jean-Jacques Spengler (Zürich) worked here.

The leading painters were Zachariah Boreman, from Chelsea, and William Billigsley.

Duesbury bought Chelsea in 1770 and Bow in 1776. King George III allowed him to carry a crown on his factory mark. Duesbury was to English porcelain what Wedgwood was to stoneware. He died in 1786. His successor, his son, died in 1796; he had taken in Michael Kean as a partner.

From 1800 to 1847 Robert Bloor was the owner, after which the factory was incorporated. Since 1935 the company has called itself Royal Crown Derby Porcelain Co. Limited.

Many famous shareholders founded this manufactory in 1751. The physician Dr. John Wall and the apothecary William Davis produced the arcana; Josiah Holdship ran the undertaking until 1772. Externally the porcelain resembled the Chinese. It was chiefly a good kind of useful porcelain with very fine blue or varicolored painting. In 1757 Robert Hancock came here from Bow, bringing his transfer process. Figures were first made here in 1769 by Tebo, who previously had been at Plymouth.

In 1772 Thomas Vernon bought the factory and reigned over Wall and David as well as the shareholders. On his death in 1776, Wall became director. Thomas Flight took over when Wall died in 1783.

The classic Flight Period lasted until 1792 when the Flight sons joined up with Martin Barr. The Flight-Barr—or Barr-Flight—Period, like one big family, ruled until 1840. Then there was great competition from a factory founded by Robert Chamberlain, a former employee. In 1848 Walter Chamberlain and John Lilly became the owners, and then from 1852 to 1862 Kerr and Binns. In 1889 and 1905 two more factories were set up in Worcester, that of Thomas Grainger and the Hadley Works, which finally merged.

1755–1790

1760–1775
1783–1792

| 1792–1807 | | |
| 1807–1840 | | |

| 1810–1820 | | |
| 1840 | | *Chamberlain Worcester.* |

1801–1812		
1812		
1896–1903		

1852		
1852–1862		
1862		

Longton Hall, Staffordshire (1750–1760)

The potter William Littler founded the factory in 1750 along with William Jenkinson and William Nicklin. In 1755 Jenkinson sold his share to the gilder Nathaniel Firmin. Robert Charlesworth was taken on later as a partner as well. A breach between Littler and Charlesworth brought about the end of production in 1760.

The porcelain was useful ware, painted and decorated in white (as were the figures). Also characteristic was a deep blue, "Littler's blue," which he developed for stoneware.

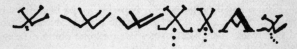

Lowestoft, Suffolk (1757–1802)

This manufactory was founded by Robert Brown in 1757, and was taken over by Walker in 1761 and by Robert Allen in 1780. It created useful chinaware for its middle-class clientele. Its blue-and-white and varicolored painting imitated both Worcester and Meissen.

Allen Lowestoft

A Trefle from LOWESTOFT

Allen Lowestoft 3 5 2

Plymouth, Devonshire (1768–1781)

The chemist William Cookworthy, a Quaker, tried for a long time to come up with a superior paste. He succeeded in discovering a hard-paste porcelain. In 1768 he set up a factory, probably using forms from Longton Hall, which had been sold off in 1760. Until 1769 the modeler Tebo worked here, then went to Worcester.

In 1770 Cookworthy transferred the factory to Bristol (Bristol China Manufactory). Richard Champion was allowed to use the patent for hard porcelain. In 1774 Champion became the exclusive owner of it. He worked from models based on Meissen and Sèvres. In 1778 he encountered financial difficulties and was compelled in 1782 to cease production and sell the stock. In 1784 Champion went to South Carolina, where he died in 1791. New Hall took over the hard porcelain patent.

In 1782 a small manufactory, New Hall, had been founded by several potters. Until 1810 it made useful tableware from hard porcelain, then went over to using bone china. Today it is called New Hall Pottery Co., Ltd.

Plymouth
1750–1752

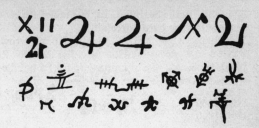

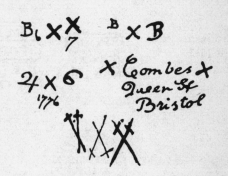

Bristol
1770–1781

New Hall
1781–1825
20th century

Stoke-on-Trent, Staffordshire (since 1770)

Josiah Spode originally made stoneware here and around 1795
bone china, which he improved and decorated by means of the
transfer process. A partnership with William Copeland proved

favorable. In the beginning of the nineteenth century they began to manufacture hard porcelain.

Josiah Spode
and his successor
1770
1784–1800
1790–1800

1790
1805–1830
1810–1833

1833–1847

19th century;
modern mark

Etruria, Staffordshire (since 1768)

The Quaker Josiah Wedgwood came from a long line of potters. From the founding of his famous factory at Etruria near Burslem in 1768 it was a great success. In 1752 he had created a new transfer process which made faster and cheaper production possible. In 1759 he created an interesting new green glaze and in 1760 he developed his famous cream-colored stoneware. A tea service of this material so enchanted Queen Charlotte that she permitted it to be called Queen's Ware. The most famous service of Queen's Ware is the great table service for Empress Catharine II of Russia, which was made in 1773–74 and was made for the La Grenouillière chateau in Zarskoje Selo near St. Petersburg. Each piece was decorated with a green frog and an English landscape. In 1768 the firm set up the Etruria factory for ornamental ware. Wedgwood's partner was Thomas Bentley, a Liverpool merchant with a great artistic interest. He died in 1780. Wedgwood exemplified the Neo-classical style which had begun to make itself felt around 1760.

In 1768 Wedgwood made a black stoneware, black basalt with reliefs in material similar to encaustic painting (baked enamel) in rust-red and and white, many totally in red. These copies of ancient Greek red figure vases Wedgwood called Etruscan Ware.

Since 1770 the firm has made great figures and busts, as well as medallions and tablets in basalt. They came out with a catalogue in 1773. Between 1774 and 1776 they created the fine-grained jasper ware, a stoneware in colors such as lavender, light blue, sage green, dark blue or olive green, bright yellow, lilac and black, with incised white reliefs. In the same style they also created cameos and plaques. White figures were colored like Sokkel and Jaspis ware. A masterly achievement, taking four years, was the copy of the ancient "Portland Vase" in black Jaspis with white figures (owned by the Duke of Portland). Besides all this they made many useful commodities, with sundry decorations, for stoves and furniture. Fine artists worked for Wedgwood, oriented toward Italy and ancient finds. Wedgwood was often imitated. In the beginning of the nineteenth century Meissen copied its decorations on porcelain reliefs and Sèvres imitated it in biscuit, often misleadingly marked.

After Wedgwood's death in 1795 the factory continued on in the same established way, using the old forms. In the early nineteenth century they created a luster decoration and about the same time they developed a fine bone china with underglaze blue painting. The business is today still run by the Wedgwood family.

WEDGWOOD

WEDGWOOD
BONE CHINA
MADE IN
ENGLAND

Italy

Florence (1575–1622)

Named by the Grand Duke Francesco Maria I de Medici, so-called Medici porcelain was made during the Medicis' reign. One of its marks, FMMDE II, means Francesco Maria (or Medici) Magnus Dux Etruriae II.

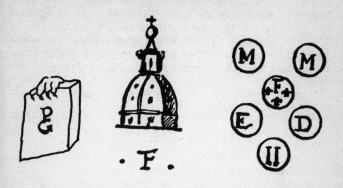

Venice (1720–1812)

Christoph Conrad Hunger went from Vienna to Venice and there in 1720 founded a porcelain manufactory along with the goldsmith Francesco Vezzi. They set up the first hard porcelain manufactory in Italy, getting their kaolin from Aue. A Saxon embargo on exports stimulated production. Hunger went back to Meissen in 1725; in 1727 Vezzi had to shut down the plant.

What was remarkable was that the underglaze blue painting was successful earlier than at Meissen. The forms of the wares leaned somewhat on Vienna and Meissen. Characteristic was an octagonal teapot with relief decor. Figures were rare.

In 1758, at the beginning of the Seven Years War, arriving from Dresden, Nathaniel Friedrich Hewelcke had a twenty-year privilege from the Venitian Senate to found a manufactory, which starting in 1763 was in stiff competition with Le Nove.

In 1765 his partner Geminiano Cozzi founded his own factory with a twenty-year privilege. He made soft porcelain (frit) with Asian painting, later conforming more to Meissen and then Sèvres. His raw materials came from Vicenza. In 1781 the stoneware was based on English models. The manufactory flourished until 1790. The occupation of Venice by the French and later the Austrians led to the factory's ruin. It was closed in 1812.

Figures of the Cozzi period are mostly unpainted. Allegorical motifs were preferred.

Vezzi

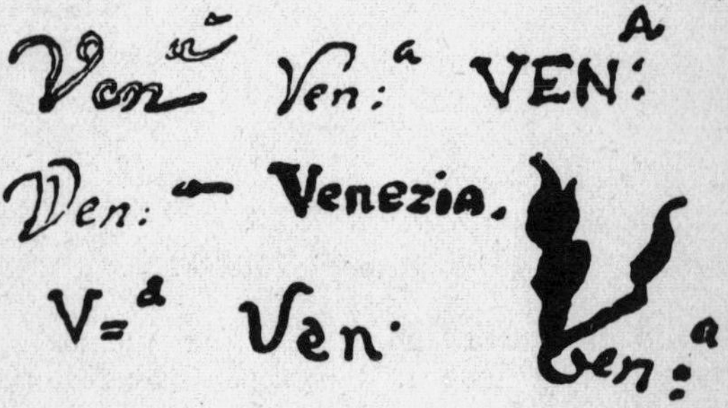

Hewelcke

Cozzi

Pasquale Antonibon ran a successful *majolica* factory in Le Nove near Bassano. With the support of his assistant Johann Sigismund Fischer from Dresden he bought a porcelain kiln and in 1762 began making porcelain. In 1773 Antonibon withdrew from the business and devoted himself to politics. By then he had been raised to the nobility. His son, Giovanni Battista, had become a partner in 1762 (mark *GBA*). From 1781 to 1801 Francesco Paolin ran the business. He worked in the Rococo style. Giovanni Baroni, who ran the factory until 1825, changed the forms and decorations over to the Empire style (mark *GB*).

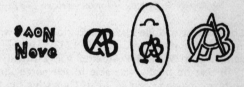

1763–1773

After 1781

NOVE. N M

G.B.
NOVE

MGS
B

Fab.Baroni Nove.

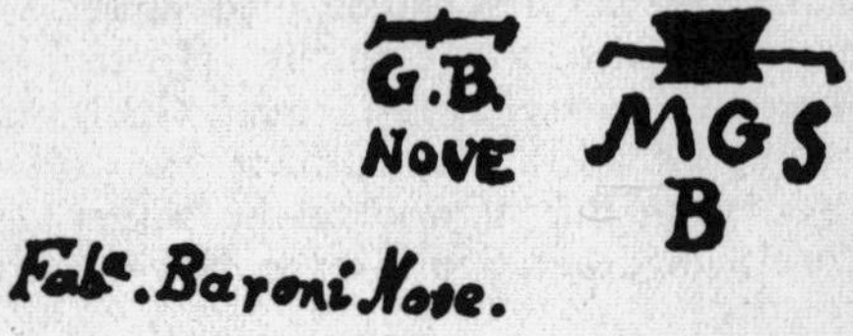

Doccia, Florence (since 1737)

The founder was the marchese Carlo Ginori, who was inspired in Vienna to make porcelain. In 1737 he engaged the Viennese painter Karl Wendelin Anreiter von Zirnfeld; it was only in 1746 that he finally was able to sell porcelain, his economic problems having been so great. Under his son Lorenzo things improved. They bought up some molds from Capodimonte on its dismantlement. The new forms were signed with a crown and an *N* underneath. This led to confusion and mixups of the two. Especially in the second half of the nineteenth century, they produced wares in great quantities and sold them to tourists as being authentically old. Almost instantaneously in Thuringia this Capodimonte ware was imitated. In 1896 Ginori and Richard of Milan merged, and set up a new factory, and today Doccia is a huge concern.

Some of their specialties were pots, cups, and fancy goods decorated with figure reliefs, created by the modeler Guglielmo della Porta (i.e., his Michelangelo group). The figure sculptures were modeled from Viennese and Meissen molds.

Capodimonte, Naples (1743–1759)

Buen Retiro (1760–1804)

Charles III, King of Naples and Sicily, had taken as consort a daughter of August III of Saxony and Poland. Therefore he was interested in porcelain. He appointed the chemist Livio Ottavio Scheppers as director and Giovanni Caselli as head painter of the royal manufactory and in 1743 erected a building and began production. Scheppers's son Gaetano knew how to improve soft paste porcelain *(pâte tendre)*. When he succeeded his father the factory became quite successful. The modeler was his brother-in-law Giuseppe Gricci and, among others, the painters were Giovanni Caselli and Johann Sigismund Fischer.

Capodimonte was important for its figure sculptures. Gricci created lively animated figures of saints and gods, shepherds and animals, as well as *commedia dell'arte* figures. The molds for china were based on Meissen and Vienna.

The mark shows various modifications of the Bourbon lily.

CC is the mark of Charles III.

Buen Retiro, Spain
1760–1804

In 1759 when Charles III was succeeded on the throne by his brother Ferdinand VI of Spain, the factory, its entire staff, appurtenances and materials were moved to Buen Retiro near Madrid. The enterprise was not entirely successful; for one thing the necessary pastes were not readily available in Spain. The manufactory produced only for the court. Then in 1804 Bartolome Sureda took over the factory's management with the help of the arcanist Vibien from Sèvres, and made hard porcelain.

In 1808 the French converted the factory to a fort and in 1812 the English destroyed it.

Among its artists were Felice Gricci, Salvatore Nofri, and C. Fumo.

Naples (1771–1834)

Charles III's son, King Ferdinand IV of Naples founded a manufactory in 1771 which made soft porcelain *(pâte tendre)* and in 1773 transferred the factory from Portici to Naples.

In 1806 French troops occupied the premises and in 1807 the plant was sold by Joseph Bonaparte to a French firm, but it was not successful. In 1834 what remained was sold off.

Above all the manufactory specialized in presentation ware for its royal clientele, besides centerpieces and figures in biscuit porcelain. An homage to Neoclassicism was its Herculaneum Service, which Ferdinand sent to his father in Spain. The Etruscan Service was a gift for George III of England. The small services reflected typical Italian motifs—the hunt, birds, and ships. The mark *RF* stands for Rex Ferdinandus. In the nineteenth century the crowned *N* was often imitated and led to further mixups with Capodimonte.

Holland

Weesp (1764–1771)

Count Gronsveldt-Diepenbroek established a *"porceleyn-makerey"* in Weesp in 1759, originally to make faience, but it was soon putting out porcelain. He was helped by Nikolaus Paul, who went to Fulda in 1764. Picot ran the factory until 1771.

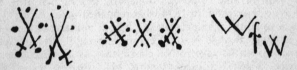

Despite the high quality of its porcelain the factory found itself in great financial straits. The pastor of the Reform Church, DeMol, took the artists, among whom was Louis Victor Gerverot (who functioned as both a worker and inventor), and set up his own manufactory in Oude-Loosdrecht.

Oude-Loosdrecht near Hilversum
(1771–1784/1814)

This manufactory was founded by Pastor Johannes De Mol in 1771.

In Schrezheim near Ellwangen, Gerverot and a few others had experimented with a porcelain kiln in an unused building until he developed a good paste. The factory produced its first piece of porcelain in 1774; by 1778 it was employing eighty-five people, including twenty-five children. The porcelain was of reasonably good quality but the factory could not hold its own against the competition from English stoneware. De Mol died, debt-ridden, in 1782. One of the creditors, J. Hope, took over the plant and sold it to Ouder-Amstel in 1784. There Freidrich Däubler was the director.

Some painters moved with the firm. It was taken over in 1800 by Donner and Co. In 1808 it was absorbed into Nieuwer-Amstel.

M:OL.   MIOL.   M:ol

M:OL   M.O.L   MoL   M.ol
           *   £m3   N°10

M:OL   M:o:L   M:OL   M:ol
L29   87J

Example of the
Schrezheim mark,
an incised lion

263

*Ð·Ð Amstel
M.O.L
Amstel*

Louis Napoleon subsidized the factory with yearly grants of 45,000 francs until 1810 when Holland became part of the French empire. The business called itself Koninklyke Porcelein Fabriek.

Oude-Loosdrecht in 1800 adopted the Empire style, using antique forms with gilt curved handles. There were few biscuit figures, groups, or busts. By the end of the nineteenth century there were no more active manufactories in Holland.

The Hague (1766–1790)

Anton Lynker started out painting porcelain solely for German manufactories in his "painting workshop," which is what he called his porcelain factory. In this way he knew he could avoid paying various customs tariffs. Finally in 1778 he financed the building of a regular plant. By the time he died there were forty employees. His widow ran the business until 1784. Their son ran it after her until 1790.

The porcelain was distinguished by good painting and gilding. Besides useful ware they painted hard porcelain for Germany (Ansbach, Volkstedt, Meissen) and *pâte tendre* for Tournay. They favored German flowers, and around 1780 they were turning out monograms with flowers and still lifes with flowers and vegetables, animals, and *putti* in purple *camaïeu*, urban scenes and medallions with heads in *camaïeu* or silhouette. They didn't make figures. Their stork was often painted over other marks (i.e., *A* for Ansbach).

The mark appears
on many pieces
in underglaze blue.
The head painter
obscured it by
overglaze blue.

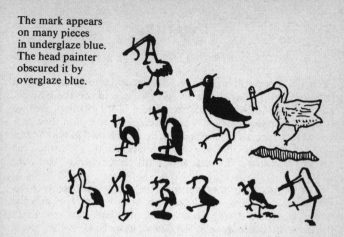

Rozenburg, The Hague (1883–1916)

This manufactory was founded in 1883 by Baron von Gudenberg with the help of Theodor Colenbrander. At first it specialized in Delft blue. In 1895 J. Juriaen Kok and the chemist M. N. Engelen tried to revive past porcelain styles. In a delicate vitreous paste, the service with nasturtiums, elders, and spiderwebs, painted by J. Stelling and R. Sterken, is one of their superior creations. Their exquisite china caused a sensation as the Paris World Exposition in 1900. The manufactory closed up shop in 1916.

Belgium

Tournay (since 1751)

François Joseph Peterinck ran a faience factory, and with a privilege from Maria Theresa and the help of the state, he began to manufacture porcelain. From 1753 Robert Dubois from Vincennes-Sèvres was the director. Under him they produced soft porcelain (pâte tendre). Peterinck died in his eighties in 1796. His son Charles ran the factory until 1799, then his brother-in-law and his son ran it until 1850 when it went over to Boch.

The factory was famous for developing veined backgrounds (décor bois); otherwise it leaned on Meissen patterns and the underglaze blue Zwiebelmuster and standard patterns. Later the decoration was done in the Sèvres style. Figures were made in white glaze and painted, or in biscuit. Figures were often arranged around a tree.

Modelers working here were Nicolas Lecreux, Nicolas Gauron, Antoine Gilles, and Joseph Willems; Henri Joseph Duvivier painted here.

Sweden

Rörstrand and Marieberg (since 1758)

In 1729 Christoph Conrad Hunger, from 1726 director of a faience factory near Rörstrand, tried to set up a porcelain manufactory. In 1735 he was dismissed for incompetency. After a short successful stay in Copenhagen he returned to Sweden and obtained a privilege for a porcelain factory, but it was soon rescinded and finally he went to St. Petersburg.

In 1743 he came up with a general paste to make ware after Chinese models. In 1758 the dentist Johann Ludwig Eberhard

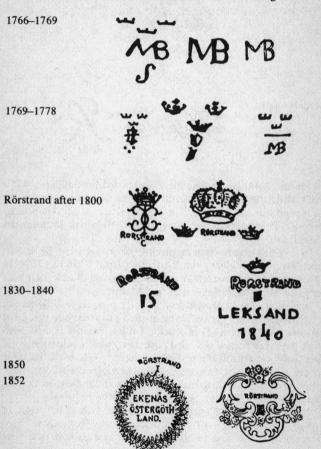

1766–1769

1769–1778

Rörstrand after 1800

1830–1840

1850
1852

1857–1860;
since 1870

Since 1884

Modern marks

Ehrenreich obtained a privilege. He started producing in 1759 even while the building was still going up in Marieberg, but all he turned out was faience. The only evidence from this period, a bowl, is preserved on view at the National Museum in Stockholm.

In 1766 Ehrenreich was discharged and Pierre Berthevin from Mennecy-Villeroy ran the factory from 1766 to 1769. He specialized in frit porcelain. At this time they based their patterns on Meissen, Frankenthal, and Mennecy.

Berthevin was interested in a transfer process for faience. In 1779 under his guidance Sèvres turned out a service using the process for Catherine II of Russia. On his leaving, Henrik Sten took over. He turned out hard porcelain, which, although quite bad, held sway until the end of the century. He used the same forms from Berthevin's time and when Neoclassicism arose with its floral painting and garlands and landscapes in rose (tone-on-tone painting), Sèvres patterns were imitated.

Not one entire Marieberg service survives. The reign of Jakob Dortu (1777–1778) produced unobjectionable hard porcelain. Dortu rose to his full powers as a painter in Berlin.

He evidently parted with none of his secrets, because when he left for Nyon the factory fell right back to turning out inferior porcelain.

In the 1780s the Marieberg factory was absorbed into the Rörstand plant. Under Bengt Reinhold Gejer, who ran the factory until 1795, they turned out stoneware after Wedgwood patterns and somewhat later brought out a wider range of porcelain ware.

Since the end of the nineteenth century, when Alf Wallander was director and created his remarkable Art Nouveau porcelain, the factory has had a reputation for good porcelain.

Denmark

Copenhagen (since 1759)

There were many false starts before a factory was established here. In 1731 the Dresden glazier Elias Vater tried, from 1730 to 1737 the Meissen gilder Christoph Conrad Hunger, around 1752 the Meissen model master Johann Christian Ludwig Glück, who came to Copenhagen from Vienna and Fürstenberg, the Meissen blue painter Johann Gottlieb Mehlhorn and the Englishman Daniel MacCarthy—all unsuccessfully.

In 1756 the rural inspector Birch discovered a suitable earth near Bornholm. In Christiania Mehlhorn founded a factory (with a blue tower) and started production, or rather tried—he was unable to make porcelain. In 1760 the factory was merged with the faience factory of Jakob Fortling; Mehlhorn died in 1761. In 1759 Louis Fournier, formerly at Vincennes and Chantilly, came to run the establishment. He was able to turn out china in hard porcelain. He knew next to nothing about sculpture. The painting was influenced by Fortling's faience factory and the floral painter Johann Georg Richter from Höchst, who in 1755 came to Copenhagen from Strasbourg.

On the death of Frederik V in 1766, Fournier left Denmark, taking with him various creative secrets of the apothecary Frantz Heinrich Müller. Müller and Richter turned out hard porcelain with kaolin from Limoges.

A new kaolin deposit was found in 1775 in Bornholm. On May 1 of the same year the Danske Porcelains Fabrik was founded. The chief stockholder was the widowed Queen Juliane Marie, sister of Duke Ferdinand of Braunschweig. A mark was selected—three wavy lines in underglaze blue, symbolizing the three waterways: the Great Belt, the Small Belt and the Öresund.

From 1766 until his death in 1795, the model master was Anton Carl Luplau from Fürstenberg. Painters came from Meissen and Berlin. The economic state of the factory was poor and the king put it up for sale. By 1779 it was called the Kongelige Danske Porcelains Fabrik. It opened a large store in Copenhagen in 1780.

Until 1784, because of Juliane Marie's influence, the factory received state support. This was the period when it rose to great artistic heights. An exceptional work was the 1776 state service for Catherine II of Russia, the Flora Danica Service, created by the painter Müller and the floral painter Johann Christoph Bayer from Nuremberg. The scientific advisor for the work was the botanist Theodor Holmskjöld.

An underglaze blue floral pattern decor with painted conch motif was very popular. In England it was called Immortelle.

Müller retired in 1802. The factory declined during the management of his successor, I.G.L. Manthy partially due to political circumstances. The Empire period began in 1824 under the directorship of G.F. Hetsch. The Berlin style strongly influenced the Neoclassic porcelain made here.

C.W. Bergsoé became director in 1833; in 1863 the manufactory merged with the Alumina faience factory; in 1867 it was taken over by private individuals. Falck bought it from the state, but was permitted to keep the name and the mark.

In 1884 Philip Schou became the owner; his artistic director was Arnold Krog. Now began a new fruitful period. Krog's painting stemmed from new developments in underglaze technique. In 1889 Copenhagen porcelain received general acclaim at the Paris World Exposition. In 1902 Schou's son-in-law Franz Dalgas took over the factory.

The present production of the Kongelige Danske Porcelains Fabrik and Fajancefabrik Alumina A/S Kopenhagen embraces models ranging from the eighteenth century to the present. Underglaze blue china accounts for a large part of present-day production.

In 1853 Bing and Grøndahl founded a manufactory in Copenhagen which artistically followed the lead of the state factory.

1759–1765

1771

1775

1830–1845

1889–1894

Since 1890

1894–1897

1897–1905

1904–1923

1923–1929

Since 1929

Bing and Grøndahl,
owned by M. Ludwig,
J. Harald Bing, and
Frederik Grøndahl

Russia

St. Petersburg (since 1744)

Czarina Elisabeth founded a manufactory in 1744. Christoph
Conrad Hunger came to St. Petersburg from Sweden to run it,
leaving because of overwork in 1748. From 1748 to 1758,
Dmitri Vinogradov was the director. He succeeded at improv-
ing and developing new porcelain paste. On his death Johann
Gottfried Müller from Saxony arrived, working as arcanist.

Up to around 1760 they created simple and small objects—
tea and coffee services and snuffboxes, mostly based on
Meissen.

1744–1762,
Elisabeth
(the signs under
the marks refer
to the clays
that were used)

1762–1796
Catherine II

1766–1782
"Anchor marks"

1796–1801
Paul I

Inventor's mark
(Pridwornaja Kontora)

1801–1825
Alexander I

1825–1855
Nicholas I

1855–1881
Alexander II

1881–1894
Alexander III

1894–1917
Nicholas II

Since 1917

Empress Catherine II gave the factory 15,000 rubles a year for its production, which was solely for her. Until 1772 it was run by cavalry lieutenant Chepotchev. He relied on the Meissen modeler Karlovski, among others. He founded a porcelain training school, hoping to encourage able young talent. Only Russian painters were available.

In 1773 Prince Viazemski took over the directorship. In 1779 he set up the French sculptor François Dominique Rachette as model master, specializing in the Neoclassic style. The chief painter was Sacharov.

Prince Iussupov became director in 1792.

In 1784 Rachette created the Arabesque Service, a center-piece for Catherine II, in which the empress was depicted amidst allegorical figures. About this time he also created the Yacht Service, which glorified Catherine's great naval victory. Rachette also made medallion portraits and a remarkable bust of the empress. Otherwise, few popular people or scenes were depicted. During the reign of her successor, Paul, who was assassinated in 1801, and then into the nineteenth century under Czar Alexander I, the output of the manufactory was converted to the style of the French Empire. During the reign of Czar Nicholas I (1825–1855), Russian peasants and other Russian types and scenes became prevalent.

The quality had seriously fallen off by the end of the nineteenth century. Then the 1917 Revolution brought with it a recovery and improvement.

Gardner Workshop Near Moscow

The Englishman Francis Gardner founded a porcelain factory in 1754 which was in competition with the czar's factory. In 1780 it was moved to Twer and in 1891 the business was taken over by M.S. Kuznetsov.

Gardner also worked for the Crown. Some of his famous pieces are the St. George Service for Catherine II, the St. Andrew Service, and the Alexander Service, all of which he sculpted and painted with medal, ribbon, chain, and star decorations. From this factory also came beautiful figures of Russian everyday life. Marks: *GARDNER* in Latin or Cyrillic script, sometimes assorted G's in either Latin or Cyrillic. In the nineteenth century, St. George, over which was an incised eagle.

We should mention the many small private factories, especially the one founded in 1801 by A.G. Popov in Gorbunov near Moscow.

Hungary

Herend (since 1839)

The manufactory was founded by Moritz Fischer in 1839. His best efforts were copies of European porcelain, which he made for the Hungarian aristocracy. Characteristic of Herend are, among others, the Victoria pattern, with butterflies and blossoms; Chinese decoration; the Rothschild Decor with twelve different bird groups painted; the Wales Decor (the service was a gift from Franz Joseph to the Prince of Wales, later King Edward VII of England); and the Fish Decor with sculpted dolphins (for the Duke of Windsor). *Siang-noir* and *Siang-*

rouge were gilded decors somewhat influenced by geometric Asian ware.

When the Vienna manufactory closed in 1864 the emperor Franz Joseph gave its models and patterns to the Herend manufactory. The *"Petersilien"* decor originally made for the Viennese crown was now manufactured in Herend.

In 1948 the firm was nationalized without changing its character.

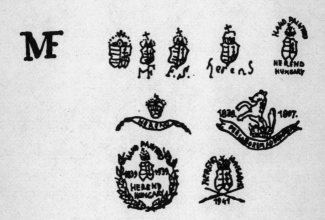

BIBLIOGRAPHY

CHINA, JAPAN, GENERAL

du Boulay, Anthony: *Chinesisches Porzellan*, Frankfurt 1963

Burton, William: *A General History of Porcelain*, London/New York/Melbourne/Toronto 1921

Chinese Porcelain of the Ch'ing Dynasty, London 1957

Chinesisches Porzellan und die übrigen keramischen Erzeugnisse Chinas, 2. Aufl. Leipzig 1923

Dexel, Thomas: *Chinesisches Porzellan*, Darmstadt o. J.

Feddersen, Martin: *Japanisches Porzellan*, Braunschweig 1960

Jenyns, Soame: *Later Chinese Porcelain*, London 1951

Jenyns, Soame: *Ming Pottery and Porcelain*, London 1953

Pelka, Dr. Otto: *Chinesisches Porzellan*, Leipzig 1921

Schmidt, Robert: *Das Porzellan als Kunstwerk und Kulturspiegel*, München 1925

EUROPE, GENERAL

Ducret, Siegfried: *Deutsches Porzellan und deutsche Fayencen*, Baden-Baden 1962

Hoffmann, Friedrich: *Das Porzellan der europäischen Manufakturen im 18. Jhd., eine Kunst- und Kulturgeschichte*, Berlin 1932

Honey, W. B.: *German Porcelain*, London 1947

Kronberger-Frentzen, Hanna: *Altes Bildergeschirr*, Tübingen 1964

Leistikow-Duchardt, Annelore: *Die Entwicklung eines neuen Stils im Porzellan*, Heidelberg 1957

Schnorr von Carolsfeld, Ludwig: *Porzellan der europäischen Fabriken, neubearbeitet von Erich Köllmann*, Braunschweig 1956

Walcha, Otto: *Porzellan*, Heidelberg 1963 (Leipzig)

Weiss, Gustav: *Ullstein Porzellanbuch*, Berlin/Frankfurt/Wien 1964

MEISSEN

Albiker, Carl: *Die Meissener Porzellantiere im 18. Jhd.*, Berlin 1959

Handt, Ingelore—Rakebrand, Hilde: *Meissener Porzellan des 18. Jhds.*, Dresden 1956

Köllmann, Erich: *Meissener Porzellan*, Braunschweig 1965

Schönberger, Arno: *Meissener Porzellan mit Höroldt-Malerei*, Darmstadt o. J.

OTHER GERMAN MANUFACTORIES

Köllmann, Erich: *Berliner Porzellan*, Braunschweig 1963

Königlich Berlin 1763–1913. Gedenkblatt zum 150jährigen Jubiläum der Königl. Porzellan Manufaktur Berlin. Herausgg. von der Direktion der Königl. Porzellan Manufaktur, Berlin

Braun-Ronsdorf, Margarete: *200 Jahre Nymphenburger Tafelgeschirr*, Darmstadt o. J.

Rückert, Rainer: *Franz Anton Bustelli*, München 1963

Ducret, Siegfried: *Fürstenberg-Porzellan*, Braunschweig 1965

Hayward, J. F.: *Viennese Porcelain of the Du Paquier Period*, London 1952

Ducret, Siegfried: *Das Würzburger Porzellan des 18. Jhds. 1775–80*, Braunschweig 1968

Schnyder, Rudolf: *Zürcher Porzellan*, Zürich 1964

EUROPEAN MANUFACTORIES

Briant, G. E.: *The Chelsea Porcelain Toys,* London/Boston (1925)

Ruscoe, William: *English Porcelain Figures,* London 1947

Wedgwood. London 1958, Small Picture Book no. 58

Les Porcelainiers du XVIIIe siècle français, Préface de Serge Gauthier, Paris 1964

Ginori Lisci, *Leonardo: La Porcellana di Doccia,* Milano 1963

Lane, Arthur: *Italian Porcelain,* London 1924

Hayden, Arthur: *Kopenhagener Porzellan,* Leipzig 1924

Ross, Marvin C.: *Russian Porcelains,* University of Oklahoma Press 1968

Boucz, C.—Gink, K.: *Herender Porzellan,* Budapest 1962

Other German Manufactories
European Manufactories

INDEX

286